T0078323

Personal
DISASTER PLANNING
Handbook

Personal
DISASTER PLANNING
Handbook

FRANK BORELLI

Responder Media books may be ordered through booksellers or by contacting:

Responder Media
1663 Liberty Drive
Bloomington, IN 47403
www.respondermedia.com
1-(877) 444-0235

Because of the dynamic nature of the Internet, any web addresses or links contained in this book may have changed since publication and may no longer be valid. The views expressed in this work are solely those of the author and do not necessarily reflect the views of the publisher, and the publisher hereby disclaims any responsibility for them.

Certain stock imagery © Thinkstock.
Any people depicted in stock imagery provided by Thinkstock are models, and such images are being used for illustrative purposes only.

ISBN: 978-1-4705-0004-7 (e)
ISBN: 978-1-4705-0000-9 (sc)

Library of Congress Control Number: 2012941043

Printed in the United States of America

Responder Media rev. date: 6/7/2012

INTRODUCTION

Oddly enough, as this manual was prepared, the East Coast of the United States experienced its first earthquake in about forty years (magnitude 5.9, epicenter in Mineral, VA, felt from southern North Carolina to northern New York) and Hurricane Irene traveled up the East Coast from August 25th – August 28th, 2011. Additionally, the "Great Dismal Swamp" in northern Virginia burned for about two weeks. Yeah... a swamp... on fire.

With an earthquake there is no warning and therefore little you can do to prepare beforehand – unless you stay constantly prepared (we'll discuss that). With a hurricane, as has been demonstrated repeatedly in recent decades, there is plenty of warning allowing for days of preparation. That preparation may end with you sheltering-in-place or with you evacuating. Both scenarios require preparation with a divergent path at some point along the way.

This manual describes a planning and preparation system which is both layered and redundant. The strength of this method is that it allows you to be both fully prepared if you shelter-in-place AND if you need to evacuate. Why would that be necessary? There are two good reasons:

First, if the disaster is an earthquake (or of similar, no-notice nature) it's likely that your preparations won't ALL be destroyed or disrupted. Given the six layers of preparation outlined, it's likely that one or more layers will survive an unexpected/unpredictable event.

Second, if you have warning, originally plan to shelter-in-place and then circumstances mandate that you evacuate, you sacrifice one layer but maintain the other five. Additionally, the other five – if maintained in a decent condition of readiness – don't require new prep time: you simply grab, load (vehicle and weapons) and go.

That line that reads "*...if maintained in a decent condition of readiness...*" is the important part. You can't simply read this manual, digest the information and then think, "Okay; I'm good to go." You must act on it and continue to do so. The most important part of disaster survival is preparation. Planning is great, but if you never act on those plans then all you've done is exercise your brain. Preparedness itself is not a one-time thing either. You must prepare and then regularly review your preparations; update as necessary; rotate equipment as required. Read this manual; develop your layers; maintain them properly; evolve them as time permits and your needs change or your ability to upgrade your preparation occurs.

That thought process was the motivating factor as this manual was written. Ironically, as mentioned, both the earthquake and the hurricane occurred during the time frame this was written. Both natural "disasters" supported the rational need for planning and preparation.

If you choose to be prepared, also be prepared for the "nay-sayers;" those who will insult your preparedness state of mind or sneer at how silly they think you are. Remember this: *Those will be the same people waiting for the government to come save them/ help them after a natural (or other) disaster occurs.* It is our moral imperative to help them as we can **without harming our family or endangering our own survival chances.** Near the end of this manual are some checklists you can use to develop your plan and track it as you complete preparations. Several of them proved handy and efficient to use/have in the past weeks.

⚠️ **NOTE:** this is not, nor is it meant to be, a manual on how to survive a complete governmental collapse, economic collapse or other events which cause infra-structure failure and anarchy. This manual is meant to offer advice and guidance on how to prepare for and survive naturally occurring or man-made disasters that are, for all intents and purposes, "short term" – meaning that you'll eventually be able to return to your place of residence. That said, even in temporary disaster situations, man's worst side tends to be displayed, so weapons for defense are discussed. Food supplies can be easily cut off, so weapons for hunting are discussed. Don't misunderstand that and take this manual to be the end-all be-all of surviving TEOTWAWKI.

If you are seeking information on planning for "The End of The World As We Know It" an excellent manual exists titled *"How To Survive TEOTWAWKI"* by James Wesley, Rawles founder of SurvivalBlog.com.

You'll note that this manual is an expansion on a series of articles published on NewAmericanTruth.com. On that same site, in the blog section, is a space dedicated to Emergency Preparedness discussion. All of your comments, thoughts, questions, observations, etc are appreciated and welcomed.

The Boy Scouts have had it right for years: ***Be Prepared!***

CONTENTS

YOU

As I sat planning this section, one of my first realizations was that everyone has a different idea of *disaster*. For some it might mean the power goes out. For others it means total government collapse and anarchy. For others still it might mean the local nuclear power plant experiences some kind of emergency that requires evacuation. For the sake of clarification, in this article as I discuss *disaster planning*, "*disaster*" means anything that is forcing you to leave your residence for an unforeseen period of time.

Now when I roll through my mental checklist for disaster planning, I prioritize what I am going to take with me and how I'm taking it with me in several different categories which we will discuss. My mode of travel is predetermined, and I've realized that my method of packing anything is layered, which we'll also discuss. First and foremost, though, I've come to realize that the level to which I can prepare for any disaster is entirely dependent on two things:

1. My own personal level of physical fitness, and
2. What level of comfort I've come to expect.

Every one of us has our own level of physical performance ability and our individual medical challenges. Some of you reading this may be so physically fit as to perform at or near Olympic levels with no medical challenges at all. Some of you reading this may be confined to a wheelchair, badly arthritic or dependent on multiple medications each day.

As you plan your disaster response and make your preparations, you have to be aware of your own physical limitations and challenges, and *you have to be honest with yourself about them.* Let me tell you what I mean: I know a man who has developed his disaster response plan entirely around his ability to hike out of his neighborhood carrying everything he feels he needs to survive on his person. I've seen his list of gear and know that he plans on carrying about 80 pounds of gear going out his door. Just to get out of the neighborhood, he's going to have to walk about five miles – and even if it's on the paved roads, there are plenty of hills. If he can't use the paved roads to walk, then he has to go through woods and streams, up and down hills and through uncertain terrain – all carrying that 80 pounds of gear.

So what's his challenge? He can't mow his yard without taking a break for a cigarette and a beer; and it's not a big yard. I'd venture to guess that, while his plan and preparation are good overall, he's badly over-estimating his own capabilities and won't be able to get off the block – much less out of the neighborhood – carrying all that. In my opinion, he'd be better off planning to use his vehicle (a large SUV) to get out of the neighborhood and not plan on hiking out until he's gotten as far as his available gasoline has taken him.

So be realistic with yourself about what your capabilities are. Developing a disaster plan and making preparations around fictional capabilities is exactly as good as not making a plan at all. If you're not in the physical shape you feel you should be (and how many of us are?), then **get to work on that**. Losing weight and becoming more physically fit is nothing more than adjusting your diet and exercising. This is something I'm intensely personally familiar with since I myself have lost over 20 pounds in the past year through nutritional adjustment and exercise.

I DO NOT mean going on some fad diet, paying a commercial weight loss program or listening to some celebrity (who is getting paid) tell you what miracle diet worked for them. I mean daily tracking your intake of food in carbohydrates, protein, fat and sodium and reducing that intake in a healthy fashion. I also mean increasing your activity through exercise at least four days each week, but six is better (I do believe in taking a day off). If you burn off more calories than you take in, then you will lose weight. It won't be ten pounds in a week, but it will be a lifestyle change that benefits you in the long run. Between the weight loss and increase in physical fitness, you'll soon realize (soon being three to six months) that your capabilities have changed and you can adjust your disaster planning around that.

Now, with personal fitness addressed, what level of comfort do you expect as you put your disaster response plan into effect? For some folks, their idea of *roughing it* means the Holiday Inn. For others it means not sleeping in a cold puddle. For some the cold puddle is an acceptable option. You have to determine what level of comfort you are going to aim for in your disaster planning and then, as you layer down your response options, recognize that each layer will reduce your level of comfort as well. While the goal is to survive the disaster in total comfort and with minimal inconvenience, the overall base goal is to survive... period. With that in mind, layer your preparation plan as follows:

- ▲ What you prepare for in your home/residence
- ▲ What you take in your vehicle;
- ▲ What you carry in a pack;
- ▲ What you carry in or on a vest;
- ▲ What you carry on your belt;
- ▲ What you carry in your pockets

I put them in that specific order because the amount you can carry to add or detract from your comfort level is reduced with each level as you go down that list. The needs you should address as you plan what you'll pack in each level must include, in some form:

- ▲ Shelter
- ▲ Food & water
- ▲ First Aid
- ▲ Defense

That may seem a short list, but virtually everything we take with us serves one of those four purposes. Moving through this manual we'll discuss preparations both for your residence as well as:

- ▲ Vehicles, concerns and load options
- ▲ Packs, concerns and load options

- ▲ Vests, concerns and load options
- ▲ On your person: belt and pockets, concerns and load options
- ▲ Defense options, concerns, legality awareness, etc.

Before you go on to read the next section, **Disaster Planning 101**, start thinking about your physical fitness and what your level of satisfaction is with it. Make the necessary adjustments NOW to benefit yourself and your family – and anyone else who might be affected by the enactment of your disaster response plan. If you need help FOR FREE, I'm using MyFitnessPal. com. It's a free website you can join, set your goals, set your current measurements and weight, and adjust how much weight you want to lose each week. It has built in databases to track what you eat and what you burn as you exercise. Remember that weight loss and increasing your fitness levels is not a short term effort; it's a marathon, not a sprint. Commit to it, start on the path, and as you do so, think about what you'd pack in your vehicle if you had to leave your residence for an undetermined amount of time.

DISASTER PLANNING 101

SHELTERING
IN PLACE

SHELTER ITSELF

When many people think about sheltering-in-place during a storm or other disaster event, they envision a single-residence house on a ¼-acre plot of land (or larger). Reality is that a large portion of our country's population lives in "high-density residential housing" such as apartments, condominiums, townhouses, etc. Another portion of the population lives in mobile homes, and some of our retired population actually permanently reside in Recreational Vehicles parked in various campgrounds. No matter which situation applies particularly to you, the basic needs are the same, and you can select the appropriate tactics described in this section as they apply to you.

> ⚠ **NOTE:** If NONE of the tactics in this section are available to you for any given survival need, *it's time to evacuate or seek new residence.* It is unacceptable to let yourself remain in a non-survivable situation for any length of time.

Whether you are in a home, townhouse, condominium, apartment or RV, the basic survival needs still have to be provided for. The biggest difference between the various types of "shelters" (homes) is the amount of space you have. For instance, if you don't have a basement, then some storage options mentioned won't be available to you. If you live in an apartment, your ability to trap and store rain water will be limited at best. Either way, you still need a water source to survive, so plan and prepare for it.

For the purposes of this manual, your "shelter" is your residence or other place where you are both welcomed and protected from nature's environment. It provides you a roof over your head, walls around you and secure windows/doors. In this section, a "shelter" is NOT a tent or other temporary enclosure where you've sought to get out of precipitation, cold or heat.

Most of us tend to take air conditioning and heating for granted. We'll discuss heating a little farther into this section, but recognize that if the power goes out air conditioning is a thing of the past. It is advisable to learn how to control the temperatures inside your shelter/residence as best you can with natural airflow. Remember that a closed-up dwelling on a hot sunny day will become a pressure cooker inside. As much as you might resist the idea, open the windows to let the air move. The shade inside is still cooler than the sun outside. Basements and other below-ground-level rooms will tend to stay cooler. During the day, it's best to keep shades drawn and blinds closed. The less sunlight you let into the house, the easier it will be to keep it cool; however, that has to be balanced against the heat produced by any light source you choose to use such as lanterns or candles.

Remember: sweating doesn't kill you. Heat Exhaustion and Heat Stroke can!

FOOD

The two biggest things to remember about food in a disaster situation, which most often involves a loss of electricity, are:

1. Cold storage will be temporary at best, and
2. Ovens/microwaves will not work unless you have a generator.

If you have any means of making fire or a cook-top heat source (camp stove, grill, wood stove, etc.) then you can boil, fry and/ or heat up most foods. Bear in mind, as was just discussed above, any heat you create inside your shelter takes time to dissipate so on hotter days you obviously would want to cook outside if that's an option. Also remember: carbon-dioxide kills. If you intend to use fire of any type to cook over, proper ventilation is an absolute must.

When you consider your food supply – think about what's currently in your freezer, refrigerator, cupboards, pantry, etc – you can identify (generally) five types:

- ▲ Fresh
- ▲ Frozen
- ▲ Refrigerated
- ▲ Canned
- ▲ Dry

FRESH FOODS include fruits and vegetables that are either just harvested or just bought. Although they will benefit from refrigeration to increase their longevity of use, they don't immediately go bad (within 16-24 hours) if left at room temperature. Cleaned, cut up and prepared properly, they provide a ready food source that is both healthy, usually high in water content and produces little waste (little to no packaging involved usually). If you have your own garden, depending on the time of year, this food source may remain available to you and be replenishable. For more information on maintaining year-round indoor gardens, do the appropriate research and make the proper preparations.

FROZEN FOODS will only remain so for as long as the temperatures inside the freezer remain at or below 30°F. Maintaining that temperature without power requires a good sustainable source of ice – also not likely without power. Recognize that anything you have in your freezer will still be usable/edible for 24-32 hours maximum. At that point, you might as well thaw it and cook it. After being cooked, if you can keep it refrigerated (45°F or colder) it should be good for another 24-32 hours. How long you can keep items frozen in your freezer also depends on how large your freezer is and how tightly it is packed. If you have extra space in your freezer, clean out and fill milk jugs, water bottles, etc. Fill them with clean water about 2/3 to 3/4 full, loosely tighten the cap and put them in the freezer. If you lose power, arrange the frozen water items around the outside and put all the frozen food items in the middle. It takes longer for a packed freezer to thaw than it does one with plenty of air space.

REFRIGERATED FOODS will have to be consumed or discarded usually within the first 24 hours. The less you open the doors on your freezer/refrigerator, the longer the cold inside will last. Although many folks freeze cooked food so that they can thaw it and eat it at a later date, it's unlikely you'll be able to accomplish this without power. Putting cooked (and therefore warm) food into a freezer will more likely raise the temperatures of the frozen items already therein than it will result in the freezing of your cooked food.

CANNED FOODS usually have a one year (or longer) expiration date stamped on them. Go look in your pantry and sort the cans. The canned goods that expire the soonest should be toward the front. The ones that have the farthest away expiration dates should be in the back. Sort them accordingly. Make it a habit when you do your grocery shopping, to put the newer items in the back. In doing this, you keep your food supply as fresh as possible and you extend the life of your larder as far out as possible. Most canned vegetables are packed in water. Many people drain that water away. DON'T. In a survival situation that water can be combined to make broth or used for soup. It CAN be consumed as it comes from the can to stave off dehydration if necessary.

 NOTE: If cans are rusted or bent/dented to the point of a fold in the metal, discard them.

"Canned foods" also includes vacuum-sealed jars of food. Although the expiration dates aren't usually as far out as those on true canned foods, they are typically out six months or more from purchase date.

DRY FOODS are items such as pasta, rice, flour, etc. Stored properly, these will last the longest. Humidity is the biggest threat to them. Typically, boiling water is the only item you need to prepare them, but if you want to flavor them in any way, you'll need to have spices, sauces, etc. available (note that such would mostly come from the canned/jarred variety of foods above). While many people don't think about it, mixing cooked pasta or rice with a can of heated up soup increases the serving capacity of the soup both inexpensively and from items that are equally well stored long term.

Heater Meals are an excellent, year+ storage capable meals.

The key, as mentioned, with dry foods is that they have to be kept dry. If you can store them in their original packaging, which typically has little moisture in it, inside of a vacuum-sealed container then most of these items will store for years. Even so, remember the rule of using the oldest food stuffs first. New items go to the back of whatever storage compartment you use; oldest comes to the front.

Not normally thought of in any of the above five categories, I consider camping food "dried food." It comes prepackaged and most often only requires you to add water to it for preparation (heated water in most cases). A look at contemporary camp food packages show that they are generally packaged as a "meal for two." In other words, if you've got a party of three, you need two packages of a given meal. They normally have a pretty good shelf life though – some reaching out as far as three years from the manufacture date.

Looking back at our list of five food types, it's obvious that disaster survival planning mandates storage of some canned/jarred foods and dry foods. If you have access to an ongoing source of fresh foods, all the better. Frozen and refrigerated foods will not be available long (48-72 hours) after any power loss occurs.

Dehydrated, prepackaged camp meals would be good to include in your pack, but work great at home too.

WATER

Make no mistake: you can live outside of shelter for weeks at a time; you can live without food for a week or more. You cannot survive more than two or three days unless you have water. A clean water source is mandatory for your survival. As such, planning to capture and secure clean water, or water than can be filtered and purified, is a priority in all survival planning.

There are a number of methods for capturing water that we probably should be using every day (just so we don't waste so much water) but we tend to ignore. Largely, in first world countries, clean drinking water is taken for granted. Unless a drought occurs, we don't even typically ration our water usage. As you read through the following suggestions for water capture and storage, note that the water is intended for different uses. The filtration and purification of water is a skill you should learn and practice if you think you might ever be without a ready clean water source for more than 48 hours.

> ⚠ **NOTE:** Most city-supplied, water-tower supplied or other "pumped in" water sources require electricity. If the electricity goes out in your area, generators and/or gravity may keep that water flowing for a couple days. After that, you're on your own.

> ⚠ **NOTE:** If you have an on-property well that pulls water via an electric pump, you can install a hand-pumped system in the water line BEFORE the electric pump. This isn't cheap but will allow you access to your well water even without electricity. Contact your local well-drilling service to inquire about the installation unless you have the necessary plumbing skills to do this. DO NOT take on this endeavor unless you're 100% certain you know what you're doing as all you may accomplish is irreparably damaging your well water supply system.

Rain barrels: Depending on where you live, not catching any of the rain runoff potentially wastes hundreds of gallons of water each year. Think about it: if one-quarter inch of rain falls onto hundreds of square feet of your roof and all that rain runs into gutters and the gutters drain into... the ground – you just lost plenty of water that could be used for watering gardens, hydrating pets, etc. By directing the gutter downspouts into rain barrels, you can capture several gallons of water per rainfall. That same water can be filtered and purified and used for cleaning, drinking and cooking. In fact, that rain water can be pre-filtered as it is caught in the rain barrels (do the appropriate internet research and construct the filtration system that goes in-line between the downspout and the barrel).

Plastic 55-gallon drums are available commercially. They can be purchased with taps already installed so that you simply have to attach a garden hose. Remember that any water captured in them will only be delivered by gravity power so it's recommended that you build a platform approximately two or three feet tall to place them on top of. Locate one under each of your gutter downspouts and don't let that water go to waste.

As the water is coming off your roof and may be mixed with leaves, shingle dust/gravel, berries and assorted other debris that lands on your roof (think about bird droppings, etc.), this water IS NOT safe to drink unless you have filtered it AND purified it by other means (boiling, treatment, etc).

TRASH CANS AS STORAGE: Plastic trash cans are also easy to use storage devices. Purchase a couple 30+ gallon trash cans and pre-place them in your basement or garage. The "cans" have to be cleaned first using either antibacterial soap and hot water OR a chlorine-based cleansing solution. Once each can is cleaned and dried, place it where you want it to stay and fill it up. Secure the lid to keep dust, animals, etc. from getting into the water. Recognize that water weighs about eight pounds per gallon, so a 30-gallon trash can full of water weighs 240+ pounds. A 55-gallon trash can full weighs over 440 pounds. That's why it's recommended that you put them where you want them BEFORE you fill them. Water can be ladled out, dipped out by bucket or cup, or you can install taps in these trash cans just like you did/could with rain barrels. IF you tap them, it's recommended that you place them a couple feet up off the ground (build the necessary platform or set them on concrete blocks) so the tap can be placed near the bottom of the trash can and you can still set whatever you're filling on the ground beneath that.

TUBS: Many folks completely forget about those plastic/metal/ fiber-glass cisterns we have in our homes called TUBS. They can be used for water storage pretty well. If you anticipate such use, clean them thoroughly with an antibacterial soap and hot water. Rinse them thoroughly as well and then fill them up! If you allow your pets to drink out of them, further filter or purify the water before using it for cleaning, cooking or drinking for humans.

HOT WATER HEATER: A ready-built, used-every-day water storage device often centrally located in your home. Holding as much as 50 gallons of water (depending on the size), every hot water heater has a tap-drain built into it near the bottom. If you need the water inside, connect a garden hose to the tap and open it up to drain the heater.

⚠ **NOTE:** It is imperative you turn off the heater before draining it. Do not assume that because the power is out you don't have to turn off the heater. Turn it off or flip off the breaker for it. When the power comes back on, a fire hazard exists unless you've turned off the power to your heater.

⚠ **NOTE:** Unless you've been without power for more than forty-eight hours consider that water coming out of the heater scalding hot and act accordingly.

> ⚠️ **NOTE:** The water in your heater is provided via your fresh water main to your house. It should be as clean as the tap water running out of your sink, shower or tub spigot. Purify, treat or filter accordingly.

TOILET TANKS: Unless you are the kind of person who keeps their toilet "drinking from" clean, none of us considers the toilet water usable. And most of us, unless we are that careful/picky, don't clean inside the toilet tank when we clean the toilet itself. The tank water is far from "clean," but it can be filtered and/or purified and used as necessary. Don't forget that it's there.

The typical toilet tank, depending on the flush system, holds anywhere from 1.6 to 3.5 U.S. gallons of water. Usually, if you need it, you'll have to ladle it out, scoop it out or siphon it out. Plan which method of extraction you'll use and make sure you have the necessary tools to do so on hand.

FILTRATION: Filtration systems of various sizes are available commercially at reasonable prices. You can get filters to fit on your tap, pitcher filters, in-line water filters or large filters capable of cleaning water gallons at a time. No matter which system or systems you choose to use, you need to insure that you have replacement filters. Given the minimum recommended water supply of one-gallon-per-person-per-day, make sure you have the means to filter/purify a sufficient supply of water for your projected need. A minimum of seven days' worth is recommended, but you can increase or decrease that based on your perceived need.

To preserve your "fine" filters to make water suitable for drinking, it's recommended that you pre-filter any water stored or collected outside, i.e. rain water captured in barrels. If the barrel doesn't have an in-line filter system that cleans the water before storage, then as you extract the water from the barrel into buckets, use several layers of clean cloth (preferably white cotton) to catch the larger chunks and pieces of debris. By doing so, you make your fine filters last longer. Additionally, if you pre-filter the rain water (as an example) you can make it potable/usable by boiling it or by using commercially available purification tabs.

> ⚠️ **NOTE:** Neither boiling water nor using water purification tabs makes it taste any better. Whatever flavor it has coming out of the barrel will be the flavor it has after purification.

POWER / ELECTRICITY

It usually takes a day or two of living without electricity before we realize and stop taking for granted the convenience of electricity in our daily lives. We use electricity nearly every waking moment for such things as heating our water (unless you have a gas-heat hot water heater), brewing our coffee, cooking our breakfast, lighting the rooms we move around in and more. Electricity is necessary to run our computers, communications tools (phones or to charge cell phones), news delivery sources (television, radio, Internet) and more. Although you CAN live without electricity, the lack of it does reduce your options for daily activities. In fact, the lack of electricity makes you focus more of your daily activities on preparation and survival.

For instance, during Hurricane Irene (August 2011) in the mid-Atlantic area, some people were without power for a week.

Their hot water heaters had run cold within the first two to three days. If they wanted warm water for cooking or cleaning after that, they had to heat the water up over a fire or on a gas stove. I know several folks who used "solar showers" (camp showers made of plastic that hold five gallons of water and use sunlight to heat the water up) starting on the third day without electricity just so they could avoid taking cold showers or "bird baths" using washcloths and heated water in a plugged sink.

In point of fact, many of the folks I know who regularly camp were less impacted, where comfort and convenience are concerned, than those who don't. Why? Because you typically don't have electricity when camping unless you have a camper with a generator.

If you perceive the need for electricity (even if it's just to keep your refrigerator/freezer(s) running), then you should purchase and maintain a decent generator. A 2500-watt generator is the minimum recommended size, and you can get them as strong as 5250 at reasonable prices. There are several concerns where generator use comes into play:

They are loud. Even the newer ones with good mufflers on them make quite a racket. If you intend to use yours at night, be polite to your neighbors and kind to yourself: build a suitable shelter to enclose the generator. If you put a latch and lock on the door, you can even use that shelter for generator storage instead of moving it in and out of your shed or garage.

They require fuel. Although the newer ones are more fuel efficient, generators still require gallons of gasoline (or other appropriate fuel, depending on the generator) to run. Not only must you plan and prepare the space for your generator, you must plan and prepare storage for the fuel.

Both the generator and the fuel are valuable commodities once the disaster has occurred, and those who didn't prepare are willing to steal to make their day-to-day lives easier. Having a secure method of storage for your generator, while it's running, is mandatory. Having a secure method of storage for your fuel supply – especially in light of the ever-rising gasoline prices we've experienced in the past decade – is equally important.

Solar power is also an option but one you have to commit to long before a disaster occurs. Additionally, the solar panels are typically mounted on the roof of your residence, and during weather events your roof is likely to take a great deal of damage. If the solar panels are up there, then they will be damaged as well. If you do have a solar power system, then the battery room (energy storage room) will hold you over for a day or two depending on how you ration out your electricity expenditure.

Small solar recharged lights can be useful and are becoming more commonplace every day. Solar charged LED lamps that are used for landscape lighting often have on/off switches and are easily twisted off their stands. During the summer months when they are being charged for twelve to fourteen hours each day, they can be taken in at night (just twist them off and take them into your residence) and will provide light for up to ten hours. If they have on/off switches, that ten hours of actual "burn" time can be spread out across 24-48 hours on a full charge if you ration out the use.

HEAT / COOKING

Electric space heaters... kerosene space heaters... propane space heaters... there are a plethora of heating options available if you have the requisite fuel to power them. Usually that means something that burns inside the containment system that is the heater. Obviously, if you have a generator, you can use electric heaters – but probably not the furnace system of your residence as it would pull too much power. Smaller space heaters are more realistic. They are difficult, at best, to use for heating up or cooking food.

Kerosene heaters provide good levels of heat provided you have the necessary stores of kerosene to fuel them. In my experience, one gallon of kerosene fuel will burn a heater for between four to six hours. If you have two five-gallon cans of kerosene (ten gallons of fuel) then you have 40-60 hours of heat. The upside of kerosene heaters is that you can often heat/cook food on the top with minimal danger. The downside is that you have to maintain them. That means completely disassembling them in the spring, summer or fall months, cleaning them, putting in a new wick and reassembling them properly. It means making sure you keep clean and fresh kerosene on hand. It means keeping anything combustible at least three feet from the heater and making sure that you don't put it on carpet or bare wood. When kerosene was $0.99 per gallon, these types of heaters were economic and efficient. Now, with kerosene closer to the price of regular gasoline ($3.50 as I type this), it's not nearly as attractive as an option.

Propane heaters, such as those designed for camping use, are compact and fuel efficient. Still, they require that you keep (and store properly) the camp-size propane tanks. Typically the design of these heaters leaves an exposed flame and you have to exercise extreme caution in placement and use.

The best solution, in my opinion, is a wood stove. Properly installed, even a small woodstove can put off enough heat to keep a 2,000 square foot house warm. The amount of wood needed to heat that size house for a period of four to seven days isn't that much. I have seen families heat their home for an entire winter on two cords of wood (about two big pick-up truck loads). You can easily cook on the top of the woodstove as well.

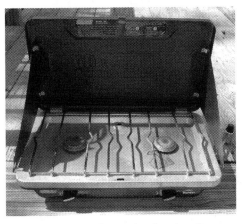

A 2-burner propane "camp stove" such as the one shown is sufficient to cook most meals, as well as heat up or brew the all important pot of coffee.

The downside of a woodstove is that you have to plan ahead to acquire, split and stack the wood so that it's seasoned and ready to use when you need it. That means the effort is year round and ongoing. The good news is that after a severe storm there are usually an assortment of trees on the ground that you can cut up, split and add to your store of wood fuel.

Care must be taken to insure proper installation of the woodstove. Furniture must be kept at the specified safe distance(s) (check the stove's owner manual for such distances), the floor beneath it and wall behind (or beside) it have to be properly insulated and protected. As great as the value of a woodstove is for providing heat and the ability to cook, the fire danger is high if the stove is not properly installed. DO NOT SKIMP on the installation. Pay particular attention to all safety warnings and notices.

PERSONAL CARE ITEMS

Throughout the remainder of this guide you'll see "CoC/TP/PT/M". That stands for:

- ▲ Change of Clothes
- ▲ Toilet Paper
- ▲ Personal Toiletries
- ▲ Medicines

Although you can't (reasonably) keep an entire change of clothes on your vest or person, you CAN keep multiple sets in your Go Bag/BackPack and/or in your vehicle, depending on how you plan out your packing. Rather than listing each of those items in each section, I'm simply going to add "CoC/TP/PT/M."

As to comments about these items:

It is a wise idea to have a full change of clothes available if you can with at least two pair of undergarments and two (or more) pair of socks. You might be surprised how refreshed you can feel simply by changing your clothes or your underwear/socks after a few days "in the field." A few baby wipes/hygiene wipes as a "bird bath" (wiping out places where your skin folds) and fresh clothes can have a huge impact on how clean you feel, how you smell and what your level of morale is.

Toilet paper: 'nough said.

Personal toiletries: Such as your toothbrush, toothpaste, soap, washcloth and a body towel. Deodorant is nice but is eventually going to become optional in a true survival situation. You have to live and stay clean – not necessarily smell fresh. If you wear contacts, make sure you take the necessary care items AND your glasses.

Medicines: Since each first aid kit should contain some type of anti-inflammatory and/or a fever-reducer, that's not what I mean by "medicines." I mean prescription drugs that you need for high blood pressure or other issues. A 30-day supply *minimum* should be packed and ready to go. More is better; however, most medicines have an expiration date, and even though it's artificially short, you should regularly rotate out your medicines that you keep packed.

YOUR VEHICLE

In the first section, (**Disaster Planning 100: You**), we discussed the importance of physical fitness and personal preparation in any disaster response plan. In **Disaster Planning 101: Shelter In Place** we took a closer look at preparing your residence as your emergency shelter. In both sections we've also looked at the layered approach to disaster planning to include what you'd load into your vehicle, pack, vest, belt and pockets. The final piece of that preparedness plan will cover weapons – which will be addressed last. In order of the items listed, in this section we'll be looking at vehicles and how you should address them in your disaster planning.

As was previously delineated, the equipment and supplies you carry, or plan on having available as you develop your disaster plan, must address some basic needs. They are:

- ▲ Shelter
- ▲ Food & water
- ▲ First Aid
- ▲ Defense

The strength of the layered plan approach is that you can maximize what you have based on which layer you are in. The layers are those listed below:

▲ Vehicle
▲ Pack
▲ Vest
▲ Belt
▲ Pockets

The last, most important and primary layer you can never get rid of is YOU.

Before we get into the considerations for a vehicle in disaster planning, let's visualize what I think of as the Disaster Planning Pyramid. From the base (vehicle), moving up through pack, vest, belt & pockets, with YOU being the pinnacle, it gets narrower. The widest part at the bottom signifies the amount you can carry – it's the largest (widest) part. As you move up the pyramid, each layer gets narrower, reducing the amount you can carry. It's important to recognize that just because you give up or lose your vehicle you don't JUST have what's in the next level (pack), but you still have a remaining pyramid of gear: pack, vest, belt & pockets and you. See the included diagram to help you understand what I'm trying to describe.

YOU
BELT+
VEST
PACK
VEHICLE

The good news about a vehicle is that you can easily carry more items to support comfortable attention to your basic needs than you can in any of the other layers. In fact, you can easily put more in your vehicle than you can in all the other layers combined. The limitations to the vehicle, though, dependent on the disaster and how far you have to travel are:

1. Travel distance limited to fuel availability.
2. Travel direction limited by terrain/vehicle type.
3. Vehicle longevity limited by maintenance supplies & your skill level.

Let's take a look at those in order.

Every vehicle made today requires some kind of fuel whether it's electric, gasoline or diesel – some mix/variation thereof. Assuming that the disaster forcing your relocation doesn't affect the national power grid, and assuming you have funding to purchase fuel along your travel route, then fuel availability isn't a problem; however, if either of those is cut, then you only have as much travel distance as your existing fuel supply will support. For most vehicles that's somewhere between 300-500 miles. You can increase that distance by having extra fuel available and transporting it with you, and there are ways to get gasoline out of underground storage tanks; however, unless the *disaster* in question includes a complete governmental and economic collapse, I will not espouse stealing fuel from underground storage tanks. Salvaging fuel from abandoned vehicles, however, is – in my mind – a wise use of abandoned materials.

Make sure you choose your vehicle with POTENTIAL terrain travel in mind. Your 2-door sports coup probably isn't the best option.

Where terrain and vehicle type are concerned, we need to recognize that your "escape" vehicle is what it is. For some of us that's a full-size four-wheel drive pick-up truck. For others it's a convertible sports coup with limited trunk space and room for only one passenger. As I've heard so often: *It is what it is*. Wishing it was something different after the fact will do you no good. Plan around what you have and improve what you have when you can. When the disaster strikes, what you have is what you had better have planned and prepared around. It's obvious that some vehicles will be restricted to traveling on paved roadways while others are better suited to rougher terrain. Think about that for a few minutes...

If you don't have a topographical map of your local neighborhood, see if you can find one online. If not, check your local outdoor supply store – they usually have some you can buy, and the terrain doesn't change that much over a few decades (unless man mechanically alters it). As you look at that topographical map, also look at a road map and figure out what your easiest route of driving travel will be... *if you can't drive on any roads*. For me and my family, that means it's a darned good thing we have a four-wheel drive Jeep with decent ground clearance. It also means that I make sure I have a shovel, chainsaw, ripsaw, hatchet and axe as part of my vehicle's disaster kit – because I anticipate having to clear some trees as we go. Will you? If so, plan and prepare.

Finally, consider your vehicle's longevity. My skill level is such that I can handle simple repairs, oil changes, etc. If the air conditioning breaks though, we're going to be using 4×55 A/C (all four windows open doing 55MPH where we can). It's called "blow through" A/C. With a Jeep, we have the benefit of being able to put the top down as well – but that robs us of shade that may be nice to keep things cool. I highly recommend, as you plan and prepare your vehicle's disaster supplies, you include a tool kit that matches your skill level as well as at least enough materials to perform two oil changes and two tire patches. If you're serious about disaster planning and you don't know how to do those two things: GO LEARN.

Now, as you plan what else you'll put into your vehicle as part of your disaster "kit," remember your priorities: shelter, food & water, first aid, defense.

Some vehicles ARE shelter if you view them that way. A quad-cab pick-up truck can easily (if not comfortably) be slept in, and it will shelter you from precipitation. If you have a cap over the truck bed, you have even more space to live/sleep *unless it's full of gear*. Outside of using your vehicle as your shelter (and some vehicles you can easily sleep under as well), you have the space/ability to carry a tent large enough to house yourself and whatever family members/ team members you plan on. My family's tent – which was designed to sleep six (in sleeping bags) – stores in a carry bag that is two feet long and one foot around. That's easy enough to pack. If you want to travel lighter than that (remembering that we're talking about your vehicle), you could consider packing a tarp with stakes and tie lines and use your vehicle as an anchor on one side.

You might be surprised what you can pack into your vehicle in a relatively small space with proper planning. All of the above gear fits in one 55-gallon sealed container. (The water jugs are packed empty in the container, but filled before loading into the vehicle.)

Where food and water is concerned, water is by far the more important AND the heaviest/most space consuming. My family has six collapsible 5-gallon jugs, each affixed with a turning tap, handle and hanger hook. If you assume one gallon per person per day (for cooking and hygiene), my family needs three gallons per day. With our vehicle we have room to carry all six jugs full providing us 30 gallons of water or ten days worth if we ration it properly. After it's used up, we'd better have a method of filtering and/or purifying more for use, right? Yes. That's why our vehicle disaster kit also includes a water filter that we can pump by hand and two sets of extra filters for it.

When you plan your food for the vehicle, you can include canned food without worrying about weight (until you're getting close to the maximum load weight for your vehicle). Remember two things:

1. The food you pack should provide a nutritional balance, and taste is a secondary consideration;
2. Your "food planning" also has to include whatever's necessary for preparation.

Few things will make you feel as silly as having pasta to cook and no pot to boil it in. Your food planning must also include preparation tools, utensils and the means to clean said tools and utensils. We have a "cook sack" that has all of our plates, cups, pots, pans and utensils in it, and we have a one-gallon ziplock bag that holds two sponges and a container of dish soap. The cleaning materials get swapped out annually, and all of our "camp kit" (pots, pans, plates, cups, utensils) get washed annually whether we've used them or not.

Next on our list of priorities is First Aid. Again, the benefit of a vehicle disaster kit is that it allows you the space to carry a large first aid kit. Even for the best trained EMT that usually means a large trauma bag. We're not looking to make our vehicle into an ambulance; our goal is to be able to patch holes, clean, close and cover lacerations and splint anything broken if necessary. How fancy your first aid kit is should be determined by two things:

1. Your level of first aid expertise.
2. The amount of money you invest in it.

My wife and I are both Advanced First Aid certified, know CPR (and stay up to date on it) and have the experience of repairing kid's injuries (as parents) for more than 20 years. Additionally I've had first aid training from the Army and throughout my law enforcement career, and we've both had first aid training directly related to SCUBA diving injuries. I don't plan on performing any act of first aid that requires me to use a scalpel. I CAN put in sutures but I'd prefer to use Crazy Glue if the cut is shallow enough and I have some at hand. But let's be honest: as good as that may be, the large majority of first aid we will need to perform will be related to small cuts, abrasions, sunburn or sprained joints. Plan your first aid kit to match your level of expertise and to fit in your allotted storage (readily accessible) space.

As far as defense goes, the largest benefit to having a vehicle is the ability to carry ammunition and maintenance equipment. Due to its weight, if you're having to carry all your ammo, there's a definite limit. Additionally, due to space (when you're carrying everything), there's a limit to what maintenance and cleaning equipment you can carry. As we're discussing your vehicle's disaster preparedness plan, you should include a "sufficient" supply of ammo for your weapon(s). (*Sufficient* is entirely subjective and you will have to determine what it is.) Additionally, you should carry whatever replacement parts you deem necessary, the tools to install them and the necessary sharpening kit(s) for your cutting tools. I tend to think of all of that as my "armorer's kit" and have it all stored as such in ONE kit – an expansive fishing tackle box that I altered / customized to suit my need.

Don't forget: CoC/TP/PT/M

DISASTER PLANNING
103

YOUR
BACKPACK

In this section we're going to discuss the next *layer*: Your backpack. Below you see the *Disaster Planning Pyramid* which allows us to easily visualize two things: first, YOU are at the top and most important; second, as you move up from the base of the pyramid you have less and less space to work with in your preparedness planning. This is an unfortunate reality we have to deal with. Where **Disaster Planning 100** dealt with preparing ourselves, **Disaster Planning 101** dealt with preparing to shelter in place, and **Disaster Planning 102** dealt with preparing our vehicles, in this section we're going to discuss how we can best make use of our backpack in our disaster planning.

Now, in every layer of our disaster planning we should address, as much as we can, our needs as related to:

▲ Shelter
▲ Food & Water
▲ First Aid
▲ Defense

Obviously, in each of those categories, a vehicle allows us more space to carry the gear and equipment that provides our needs and imposes fewer restrictions on weight; however, now that we're discussing our backpack, there are definitely space and weight restrictions. The space limit is delineated by your pack and all its pockets/pouches while the weight limit is delineated by YOU; your physical fitness level and strength. The importance of fitness was well discussed in **Disaster Planning 100,** so if you haven't read it, I'd suggest hopping back to it, reading it and then coming back to this section: **Disaster Planning 103: Your Backpack**.

Your first step is (obviously) to choose that backpack you will use as part of your disaster response preparedness kit. Quite often such packs/bags are referred to as *Bug Out Bags* or *Go Bags*

The Hurricane Pack from ASAP comes prepacked with all of the necessities two people would need for three days.

or *Get Out Of Dodge Bags* (GOOD Bags). I've previously written about them, updates about them, etc. There is a complete list of those online articles in **Disaster Planning 110: Online Resources** along with a list of articles and reviews that may be of use in your disaster planning.

As I was saying, your first step is to pick out your pack. There is a huge selection to choose from that allows for size, colors, camo patterns, integrated hydration systems (or not), MOLLE webbing on the outside (or not), etc. Your two biggest concerns as you select your pack should be:

1. Will it hold all that you plan to carry with room to spare (because you never know what you'll have to unexpectedly add), and
2. Can you comfortably carry it?

Some of the biggest names in backpack manufacturers make packs that are (to me) damned uncomfortable to wear and carry. Should you use such in your disaster response planning kit, then you're stuck with it and all of the discomfort that comes with it. Select wisely.

A good pack will have padded adjustable shoul-

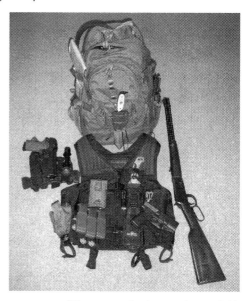

When you realize how much you might have to carry for an unknown distance or period of time, the comfortable fit of your pack becomes paramount.

der straps as well as a padded adjustable and removable waist belt. Next I would suggest to you that a good "bug out bag" must have a storage capacity of **at least** 2,000 cubic inches – and preferably more if you can carry the weight. My first Bug Out Bag was a BLACKHAWK HydraStorm Force 5 pack that had 2,240 cubic inches of space. I was amazed at what I could put in there, but realistically speaking, it was all necessary. If you decide to get a pack that has MOLLE webbing on the outside of it, you can create a modular Bug Out Bag that has even more space – again, if you can carry the weight. And I need to put in a word of caution here: Don't create a Bug Out Bag that is so heavy you can't carry it. In doing so you'll only restrict yourself to either leaving it behind or traveling very short distances at each movement interval.

The next biggest concern in planning what you put into your pack is to realize that, due to space and weight constraints, you can't carry as many days worth of supplies. Whereas, as I described in **Disaster Planning 102**, I can carry ten days worth of water for my family in my vehicle, I am limited to carrying a whole lot less in a pack. Which brings up a good point some folks forget about: every person in your party should have their own Bug Out Bag. In my home that means one for me, one for my wife and one for my son. **Each** of them is prepared as described so that none of us is carrying the weight of the other, although we do divide up some common needs between the packs. In general, each Bug Out Bag is a "stand alone" bag that will support the person it was built for over the span of three days.

Given the space limitations of the pack, *shelter* will likely be limited to a tarp, poncho, small pup tent or bivvy tent (single person). If you choose to use a tarp or poncho, make sure you include the necessary stakes and tie lines. Also, recognize that the same space limitations in the pack may restrict you from carrying much in the way of additional outer clothing, so if you don't already have on a jacket or coat, a hooded sweatshirt may be the best you can do in additional clothing. For warmth as part of your *shelter* considerations, make sure you include an "emergency space blanket" (they also now come as bivvy sacks which is like a sleeping bag without the part that goes around your head) and fire starting materials.

Four small stakes, several feet of 550 cord and a surplus poncho is all you need to make several types of shelter. (see the next page)

Your water carrying capacity will likely be limited to the hydration system incorporated into the pack (if there is one) and/or any canteens you can carry. If this is all the water you have available to you, rationing it becomes mandatory. As mentioned in **Disaster Planning 102,** the usual amount of water per person per day for cooking and hygiene is one gallon. Most hydration bladders – the largest ones anyway – hold about 100 ounces/3 liters of water. One gallon equals 3.78 liters, so that 3 liters isn't even one day's worth of water if you use the "one gallon per day" ration. Additionally, since you can only expect that 3 liters of water to last you two days (at most and if you really stretch it out), you **HAVE** to have another means of purifying water for your use whether it's a filtration system, treatment tablets, or something else. Bear in mind that whatever your system is for purifying more water, you need one such system for each person.

One poncho, four stakes and a few feet of 550 cord and you have an "instant" pup tent. Downside: It's open at both ends... but it's shelter from precipitation and will block some wind.

Food is easier and less fun all at the same time. The number of days worth of food you can carry is limited in direct proportion to the form you carry it in. What I mean is that you can carry a lot more dehydrated food than you can hydrated food. It's easier to carry MREs than it is to carry canned food equal to the same number of meals. If you take out the idea of "meals" and simply focus on nutrition, it's even easier to carry the supplement bars than it is to carry MREs. With each step down, though, you lose flavor and pleasure in eating. Remember that in a survival situation you'll be eating for maintenance, not pleasure.

Your first aid supplies in a backpack are also more limited by space. At this point you need to start measuring your perceived greatest risks and tailor your first aid supplies to them. Obviously things like band-aids, ibuprofen and ace bandages are necessary, but how about inflatable splints or cravats for slings? Do you need a tourniquet (or two) and some pressure bandages? What do YOU perceive as your greatest threats, and what potential injuries do YOU see the need to prepare for? It's okay if you're wrong – the only person you'll answer to is YOU; just like the only person who will suffer if you're wrong is YOU. Of course, when you're building first aid kits for multiple Bug Out Bags (such as I did for my family), you're able to include more options in supplies and spread them out among the kits. A word of caution though: Make sure you know where to find what you need in a hurry: some injuries aren't time friendly.

After you've made sure that those four priorities are addressed as you've packed your Bug Out Bag, then you can add in other items that I consider mandatory but are dependent on space available:

- ▲ Extra ammo
- ▲ Maintenance equipment/tools
- ▲ Navigation materials
- ▲ Lights
- ▲ Rope

Don't forget: CoC/TP/PT/M

In **Disaster Planning 104** we're going to look at equipment vests and what you can put in them just in case you have to leave both your vehicle and your pack.

DISASTER
PLANNING
104

YOUR VEST

In the previous sections of this manual we've looked at the shelter-in-place, vehicle, and pack layers, the pros and cons of each and how they can/should work together when the caca hits the oscillating rotator. In this section we're going to look at the next layer up on the Disaster Planning Pyramid: **Your vest**. If you already have one, then we're going to discuss what you should be thinking about stocking it with. If you don't have one, then we're going to discuss your selection process, how you set it up and what you should be thinking about stocking it with. Let's dive in...

If you don't yet have a vest then you have, essentially, two choices to make as you shop for one:

1. Do you want a vest strictly to carry equipment? or do you want one that is a body armor carrier? and
2. Do you plan on using it for survival gear? or will you set it up to support your defensive weapons? or both?

Think about that first question because how you answer it will determine how much money you have to spend to get what you seek. A good soft body armor vest can run you well over $1,000 or as cheap as $350 – remembering that you get what you pay for. Additionally, body armor definitely increases the weight of the vest and usually makes it more cumbersome to put on and take off. If you want the vest strictly to carry equipment, then your cost can be as little as $50-$60 for an acceptable quality vest, or upwards of $400-$500 if you want to go completely modular and customize it to suit your needs.

Some commercially available vests come with preplaced pockets for you to load. This might work well for you.

Only you can make those decisions, and they need to be made before you make a purchase. At a bare minimum, I recommend that you get an equipment vest that has multiple pockets on the front and sides but has a blank back. Although, in **Disaster Planning 103: Your Backpack** we discussed having your hydration system integrated into your pack, it's also good to have it at least as an option in your vest. Whether or not you use it is up to you. I happen to believe that redundancy is good and, if you have the hydration system in your vest, if you have to ditch your pack, you still have water with you. The other side of that is this: if you fill both hydration systems – the one in your vest and the one in your pack, you have 6 liters of water between your back and the pack. Water shifts, holds heat, etc. You have to measure the comfort for your consideration.

YOUR VEST FOR SURVIVAL

If your intention is to use your vest to carry survival gear, then you still need to address the four basic priorities within the limited space you have available:

- ▲ Shelter
- ▲ Food & water
- ▲ First Aid
- ▲ Defense

Remember that you're working with a far more restricted space, so what you carry to address *shelter* may be limited to a space

blanket or space bivvy, or it might include a carefully folded poncho carried in what's usually referred to as a "map pocket" (a flat mesh pocket) inside the vest. No matter which of those options you choose, I also recommend you carry an emergency poncho in one of the vest pockets.

Author's vest, full frontal view. The back is kept blank so his pack doesn't rub on anything.

You can get these things in clear, yellow or orange for about $2 or less at most outdoor stores and gun shows. Get a half dozen or more and spread them out in your kit: your vehicle, your pack, your vest. You may even consider putting one in a utility pouch on your belt or include one as part of the items you stuff your pockets with in the event of an emergency departure from your residence. Think of them as a personal tent that you can sit in or under to stay (mostly) dry and that will help retain your body heat, especially if you're wrapped in a space blanket under the emergency poncho.

> ⚠ **NOTE:** Don't mistake this emergency poncho as the same thing as the surplus military poncho I've previously mentioned for use as a shelter. The emergency poncho is nothing more than a cheap plastic poncho made for one or two uses at most.

Author's vest, right side: small pouch holds emergency blanket & emergency poncho. Large pouch is for food, spare batteries and other necessities.

Where food and water are concerned you, again, are limited to what you can or can't carry. For water you have two basic options: a hydration system integrated or a pocket/pouch to carry a canteen or water bottle. A large hydration system will carry about 3 liters or 100 ounces of water – just shy of one gallon. In-line filter systems are available but should not be depended on exclusively to make your drinking and cooking water clean. I'd still recommend boiling or otherwise purifying the water before putting it into the hydration bladder (after it's cooled). Canteens and water bottles are certainly better than not having any water at all, but they are cumbersome and create an imbalance to carry. In fact, if you're going to use canteens I'd recommend mounting them on your belt behind each hip – something we'll discuss at greater length in **Disaster Planning 105: Your Belt.**

For food, unless you have a really big pouch or pocket or carry an MRE, you're limited to supplement bars. Protein bars will work well, as will granola bars, etc., but to really get a good nutritional mix in as compact a package as possible you need to seek out and stock survival bars. A number of companies manufacture and sell these, and each company will give you a good reason why theirs are the best. In general, they're all good and will support your nutritional needs. Several of the better ones recommend consumption of one bar per day, and I'd suggest you put <u>at least three</u> in your vest; six would be better if you have the space. Plan what you'll carry for food as if you're going to have to scrounge or hunt once what you've got is gone... because you may well have to.

For first aid, given the restricted space, we have to reduce what we carry to the necessary supplies to treat more serious injuries. Whether we like to admit it or not, most scratches, scrapes and lacerations will heal without us putting band-aids on them. So rather than packing band-aids, put a dozen butterfly bandages in your vest's First Aid Kit. I'd also suggest making sure you have some antiseptic wipes (six to twelve), two pressure bandages and at least one tourniquet. If you are familiar with the use and health concerns of hemostatic agents, such as QuikClot, then I'd recommend including that as well. QuikClot gauze is, in my opinion, a happy compromise because it can be used both to pack deep lacerations and to wrap limbs with long lacerations. Make sure you include a "travel tube" of your preference in pain-killer/anti-inflammatory such as Motrin or ibuprofen. A small suturing kit can be included to include the needle and a limited amount of silk/thread.

That leaves us with defense, and if you're focusing on survival supplies in your vest, then what you dedicate to supporting your defensive weapon systems will be limited. Without having determined what your defensive tools will be, it's impossible for me to make any recommendations about what you should be carrying in that regard on a survival-gear-focused vest. I DO recommend that, somewhere on there you have a knife sharpening tool; ceramic sticks, diamond stick, stone... whatever you're comfortable with and have room for. Your knife is probably your most important survival tool. Being able to keep it sharp is mandatory.

YOUR VEST FOR DEFENSE SUPPORT

A vest for defensive support is far easier to discuss and describe. Much to the surprise of many folks, though, you still (normally) incorporate hydration and first aid concerns. As much as you're using the surface space of the vest for extra ammo, cleaning equipment, knife sharpening tool(s), etc., the hydration pocket is still there and doesn't really have another use related to defensive actions/items – so use it for hydration.

Since you can't really discuss using weapons for defense without recognizing the possibility that you will get injured by a weapon as well, the first aid requirements remain. The supplies I'd recommend here are the same as those listed above. You need to be able to clean and close lacerations, patch holes and stop bleeding. Butterfly bandages, pressure bandages and a tourniquet are necessary. If you have the skill required, include the suturing supplies.

Beyond that, you'll need to make sure you have the ability to carry spare ammunition, in magazines or in loops for your primary and secondary defensive weapons (discussed at greater length in the appropriate section). If your primary defensive weapon is a shotgun, bolt action rifle or lever action rifle, then you'll need the appropriate ammo pouches with loops to hold your spare ammo. If, on the other hand, your primary weapon uses magazines to feed ammo, then you'll need the appropriate pouches to hold your predetermined supply of magazines. I've long been a believer in the *standard infantry load out* where magazines are concerned: that means one in the rifle and six extras. Depending on the weapon, magazine size, width, length and

Author's vest left side: light, knife, multi-tool (in knife sheath pouch) and two magazines for his sidearm.

your stature, you may be able to carry more or less. I strongly recommend you also carry at least two spare magazines (or speed-loaders?) for your secondary weapon (handgun).

Bear in mind, in that previous paragraph, I'm assuming that your primary weapon is a rifle or other long gun and that your secondary is a handgun. If that's not the case, if your primary defensive weapon is a handgun, then you need to up your count for spare magazines. At a minimum, add together what I've suggested for primary and secondary and make them all for your handgun if it's your primary defensive weapon – a total of eight spare magazines on your vest. Make sense?

As you'll see in the next section, spare ammo/magazines for your secondary weapon will also be included on your belt and any platforms you may add.

Don't forget: CoC/TP/PT/M (Change of Clothes not likely due to restricted space. Do the best you can.)

DISASTER
PLANNING
105

YOUR BELT
& POCKETS

Never leave the house without a knife, a gun and a lighter. That was what my Uncle Don told me in 1977. It is Borelli's Rule #5 (article available online). When I asked Uncle Don to clarify why those three items, his answer was quite succinct: *That way you can kill food, clean food and cook food.* It made sense to me. In this section, as we look at those items you need to have on your belt or in your pockets if you're forced to leave your residence due to a disaster, please understand that each item listed serves a distinct purpose. I will do my best to articulate the reasons for each item, the use and need I see for it and why I carry it where I carry it – or at least plan to.

Before I go further, I have to add this caveat: *Where I discuss weapons, it is the responsibility of you, the reader, to insure that you comply with all laws of your municipality, county, state and federal system before and while carrying*

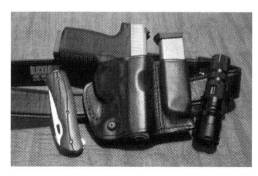

Author's typical "EDC": Kahr CW4543, spare magazine, light & knife. More in his pockets.

any weapon. In the course of this section we will discuss, at a minimum, knives and handguns, so be aware that, where recommendations are made, you need to heed them in compliance with the laws that affect you. That said, in a true disaster situation, you need to evaluate the application of said laws and act in accordance with your own best judgment and interests.

⚠ **NOTE:** In apparent disregard for the 2nd Amendment and the applicable state laws, various politicians have, during times of weather emergencies, either suspended the Concealed Carry Permits of their state (North Carolina during Hurricane Irene) or ordered the confiscation of privately owned firearms (New Orleans during Hurricane Katrina). Although I cannot advise you to violate any law or state order, I cannot fathom relinquishing or not carrying on my person my only means of personal defense in a disaster situation. History and case law have long proven that neither the federal government, any state, county or municipal government has any responsibility for our personal safety. Only YOU are finally responsible for your personal safety. Make the appropriate decisions and act accordingly.

In this section we're going to discuss what you need to carry...

- ▲ in your pockets
- ▲ on your belt
- ▲ on platforms that can be attached to your belt

As we've discussed in the previous sections, the items you need to address, as much as you can at each layer of preparation, are shelter, food & water, first aid and defense. The limited space available on a belt and in your pockets obviously limits your options in addressing each of those needs. That's not to say, however, that you can't adequately prepare yourself IF you have planned and prepared. If all you have to grab is a properly set up and equipped belt, along with what's in your pockets each day (if you're anything like me), then you'll still be able to produce or enhance shelter, eat for a couple days, patch minor injuries and/or bullet holes/lacerations, and provide for your defense. Let's discuss what you can have in your pockets, and then we'll take a look at what you can add on your belt and on platforms that attach to your belt if you choose to exercise that option.

IN YOUR POCKETS

As a matter of daily practice, I always have a few items in my pockets. They include:

- ▲ My wallet – identification will be mandatory no matter what happens
- ▲ Folding knife (or knives)
- ▲ Zippo lighter
- ▲ Flashlight
- ▲ Keys
- ▲ Cell phone

Survival items addressed: (potential) defense (knife or knives) & flashlight; warmth (lighter to make fire). General preparedness: flashlight and cell phone.

Just day to day I believe in carrying a folding knife, a lighter and a small flashlight of some kind. The need for a wallet and keys is obvious. Many of us work in buildings where we are dependent on electricity for light and we take for granted that, if the power goes out, emergency lights run by batteries will come on. That's an assumption that may, quite literally, leave us in the dark if either the emergency lights are broken or the batteries are dead/ bad. Even a small 10-lumen LED light will provide sufficient illumination to navigate to a stairwell and find your way out of the building. Brighter is better, and there are some really convenient-to-carry lights that are pretty powerful. The Extreme Beam Alpha-Tac and the Brite Strike EPLI are both perfect examples. (See review links in the resource section at the end of this manual.)

The knife you choose to carry can be conveniently sized and still have strong cutting capability. I recommend a folding lockblade knife (liner lock, Axis lock or lockback is fine) with a blade anywhere from 2″ to 4″ in length. Since the knife grips on a folding knife are usually 1/2″ to 1″ longer than the actual blade length, if you go much longer than a 4″ blade you get a folded package that becomes inconvenient to pocket unless you wear pants with pockets specifically designed for such (more on such apparel momentarily).

There are some knife designs that incorporate more than one feature into a small package. The SOL Core Lite from Adventure Medical Kits has a smaller blade than I prefer (about 1.75″) but the handle has a built in LED light and a signal whistle. The clip lets you carry it easily in your pocket, and the 3.5″ overall length means you don't have to use the clip if you don't want to. Other knives incorporate different survival features such a fire-starters, lights, whistles, rope cutters, gut hooks, etc. The more performance features you can get out of a *quality* design, the better your chances are of having the tools you need when an emergency happens or disaster strikes.

The lighter may seem ridiculous to some, and, in fact, some may be opposed to it because they mentally connect it to smoking.

Further, if you live in a city, why would you need a lighter to make a fire? Heat and shelter are all around you, right? Yep. Right. Maybe…

What if that emergency or disaster means you have to leave the city? Where is your heat and shelter? It may be your vehicle, but how do you cook? Aside from creating the knife as a tool, being able to build and control a fire for heat and cooking is one of man's defining evolutionary moments. If we as contemporary technologically adept humans disregard the value of "the old ways," then we doom ourselves to total dependency on electricity and technology. Power goes out. Batteries fail. Ovens and stoves break. No matter how weird it may seem, and even if you never need it, put a lighter in your pocket. They're cheap and don't (usually) go bad.

Now, as I mentioned earlier, some pants have specific pockets designed in for knives, lights, phones, etc. There are several manufacturers who make pants and shirts with either hidden or expanded pockets or additional pockets designed to carry miscellaneous gear. If you have or acquire such apparel, then you can plan what goes in each cargo pocket, knife pocket, etc. Wearing such pants, if properly fit and planned, will enable you to carry the necessary supplies both for shelter and food as well as spare ammunition if necessary. ONE cargo pocket is big enough for six or more nutrition bars – which, if rationed, can provide you with the necessary caloric fuel for a day (each bar). Shelter can consist of an emergency poncho and an emergency "space blanket" or bivvy. Even the cheap plastic emergency poncho can be tied up, tacked up, or otherwise spread over you to protect you from the rain. If it's not clear (plastic), it can also afford some amount of shade.

ON YOUR BELT

Most folks today put some kind of carrier or pouch on their belt for their cell phone. Most of the people I know who can legally carry a firearm put a holster on their belt along with a pouch for at least one spare magazine. Some of my friends also put a folding knife (in a sheath) on their belt, a flashlight (in a pouch) on their belt and/or a multi-tool in its sheath on their belt. If you put all that stuff on your belt, then you leave plenty of room open in your pockets for other supplies; however, when planning what you'll put on your belt for disaster preparedness purposes, I'd suggest you also consider putting a small first aid kit on your belt where you can easily reach it and that you think about a small "survival" kit as well.

One thing that I would be sure to include on my belt (in an emergency evacuation/disaster situation), no matter what you've previously planned in your pack, on your vest, or in your vehicle, is a good fixed blade knife. It doesn't have to be huge; it doesn't have to be a "survival" knife. It does need to have a blade between 4"-6" long and be in a sheath that holds it securely. When I say "securely," I mean if you were hanging upside down, the knife wouldn't fall out. The spine of the blade can be toothed or not (I like true kerf cut saw teeth, but that's hard to find) and the sheath can have a pocket/pouch for a sharpening stick or stone. Consider this knife your utility knife: cutting cord, string, line, nylon webbing, etc. It may also need to cook or stir your food, so maintain it appropriately.

The first aid kit need only hold a small "travel" tube of pain killers/anti-inflammatories (Motrin, ibuprofen, etc.), a half-dozen band-aids, a small tube of antiseptic, two pressure

The belt you use as part of your "system" can be a pants belt, gun belt or other belt you've chosen that suits your needs.

bandages and one tourniquet. If you have the skill, throw in a suture needle and some silk or thread. Understand that as I recommend those contents, I'm focusing on a first aid kit that you can use to treat *yourself*. Those items can be fit into a relatively small pouch, and there are a number of companies which manufacture "utility" pouches made to be worn on your belt and of various sizes to suit your need.

In a *survival* kit (also carried in one of those pouches) you can include an emergency poncho, emergency space blanket, fish hooks and line, matches, a P-38 (collapsible can opener, some have spoons on the handle end), and more. How big or small you make it is entirely up to you. What you put in it should be based on your needs to address the basic survival/disaster preparedness concerns: shelter, food & water, first aid and defense.

Finally, many of you may have seen war movies wherein the soldiers were carrying two one-quart canteens on their belt, with each canteen riding just behind each hip. That placement accomplished a couple things: it allowed the soldiers to carry two quarts or 1/2 gallon of water (to start out); it spread the weight of that water (about two pounds per quart) out on their waist; it allowed room between the canteens for the backpack to ride so that the weight of the pack wasn't pressing the canteens down or uncomfortably apart. If you choose to put hydration on your belt, I recommend this system. Nalgene one-quart canteens are readily available as are the carrier pouches for them. If you choose to do this, also look around for a surplus (or new) aluminum canteen cup. This cup is about half the size of the canteen itself and has fold out handles. You can use it to boil water in if necessary, mix soup, etc. The cup fits onto the bottom of the canteen and then the whole unit goes into the carrier pouch. Buy two cups... redundancy is good. Actually, maybe a better rule is this: have a canteen cup for every 1-quart canteen and an equal number of canteen pouches.

IF YOU ADD PLATFORMS

Several companies today make "tactical" or thigh platforms. Although originally developed for mounting holsters on, these platforms are typically MOLLE compatible, adjustable as far as where they ride on your thigh, and some even offer the option of carrying a body armor insert. Every kind of pouch you could get to mount to a MOLLE vest, you can get to mount on these platforms. The only real restriction is that the pouch can't be (much) taller or longer than the platform you're mounting it on. You have to roughly have the same number of MOLLE straps on the platform as you do on the back of the pouch you're attaching.

The addition of platforms to your belt "system" allows you to accomplish two things if you'd like:

1. It allows you to get the gun down off your waist. This is especially useful in vehicles if you need to access the weapon quickly and when sleeping since you can usually adjust the platform to the front, side or back of your thigh depending on how you're laying.
2. It allows you to mount pouches either for first aid, survival, or ammunition – or anything else you feel is mandatory – without tying up belt space around your waist.

That second point is important. Using myself as the example, I have a 34″ waist. That's 34″ of "real estate," minus belt loop spaces and buckle space, to carry items on. If I move my handgun down onto a thigh platform, I free up that three or four inches of space on my belt. If I move my first aid pouch and my survival kit down to the opposite side platform, I free up about ten inches of space on my belt. Now things that I might have had to put on the back of my belt, which would have been pretty uncomfortable when I was carrying/wearing a backpack, can be moved around to the sides or front of the belt. Additionally, on the same platform where my handgun is now holstered, I can mount a sheathed knife, extra magazine pouch or flashlight pouch if I deem it necessary. The addition of thigh platforms is, essentially, like getting 14 to 16 extra inches of space "on your belt."

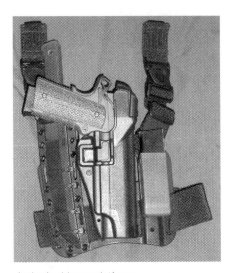

Author's sidearm platform:
gun, knife, spare magazine

With all that said, don't just rush out and buy two thigh platforms, a holster for one, pouches for the other and put everything together without further thought. You need to think of your pants, belt and platforms as a *system*. If you're going to put bulky supplies in the cargo pockets of your pants, then the thigh platforms have to be adjusted to ride above or in front of the cargo pockets. If you're going to use two thigh platforms, make sure that you don't fill up the room on your belt where the platform straps need to be secured. Make sure that your belt is a quality leather or nylon belt and that it's not worn out. It would present another challenge if the belt you had counted on to carry the weight of everything on it and the platforms wouldn't even hold up your pants because it's worn out and breaks ten minutes after you grab all your disaster preparedness gear and head out.

Don't forget: CoC/TP/PT/M – as much as you can given the limited space you'll be working with.

In the next section we're going to discuss defensive weapons. Throughout that section, you may need to refer to this and the previous sections for information about where and how to carry spare ammo, maintenance equipment, etc.

DISASTER
PLANNING
106

YOUR WEAPONS

This section about weapons has two very specific slants to it: one, examining weapons for defense, and the other, examining weapons as hunting tools. As you read through it, some of the weapons mentioned may not make sense for one of the applications but may make sense for the other. Although I don't discuss weapons as offensive weapons (tools of aggression), obviously some of them are designed for that. Ultimately, how you use any weapon is your responsibility and only you can justify it. That said, let's take a look at the various weapons/types listed below, some strengths, some weaknesses and some options.

SHOTGUNS

The potential versatility of shotguns, thanks to the ammunition availability, makes them highly valuable in my estimation. Although I do have experience with semi-auto shotguns, my preference is for a pump action shotgun (I've had my Remington 870 for over 30 years now) for several reasons. Simplicity is one of the pump shotgun's greatest strengths. They are relatively easy to understand in function, field strip, clean and reassemble. Pump action shotguns are easy to load, easy to operate and easy to unload.

Shotguns are not small though, and there is no hiding one; however, they are easily recognized by anyone who has ever watched television or movies, and they are generally thought to be devastating weapons. The sound of the action working is almost universally recognized and will make bad guys think twice about attacking. (That action-rack sound just isn't the same with a semi-auto, and I do put some value on the psychological impact that sound has.)

Ammunition versatility (as mentioned) is also a strength of the shotgun. With ammo types ranging from slugs (single projectile) to twelve-shot (LOTS of small pellets), changing ammo can alter the purpose of the shotgun. For example, if you're using it as a defense weapon, 00 buck (nine .32 caliber pellets in a 2.75″ shell) might be best, but if you're hunting squab for food, then 8-shot (or smaller) would be better. For disaster situations, I prefer a shotgun without a choke, but different folks like different things. Anything that limits your weapon use should be avoided for crisis planning and preparation. If you, for whatever reason, feel the need to have less-lethal capability, you can get home defense shotgun ammo that is designed for that purpose. You can also get twelve gauge flares, "pepper blasters" (pepper mace rounds), and more. In fact, there is such a plethora of ammunition designs for the twelve gauge that your bigger challenge may be figuring out how to prioritize what you need and how to place it.

Capacity is one challenge of the shotgun. With a standard tubular magazine holding five rounds or less, you either want to be real good at reloading or you have to plan accordingly. Shotguns set up for hunting (in most places) have a three-shot maximum capacity. *Defense* shotguns can be expanded though: mine has a 7-shot tubular magazine, a 5-shot "side saddle" shell holder and a 6-shot "power pack" (from Knoxx Stocks, part of BLACKHAWK Products Group) on the stock for a total of 18 rounds available in or on the weapon itself. Using a MOLLE thigh platform and two 18-round shotgun ammo holders from BLACKHAWK, I have 36 rounds more in a single location that is easily carried if we need it.

A sling is almost mandatory for any large weapon (which the shotgun is, and more ammo can be put on the sling in bandoleer fashion) because otherwise you're permanently committing one hand to carrying the weapon. That's better than not having it at all, but the ability to sling it and have both hands available for other work is preferred. The after-market shotgun accessory business is booming, and you can "dress" your shotgun however you prefer. If you add anything to or modify your shotgun, make sure you practice with the new configuration. If you add a light, remember that you need replacement bulbs and batteries – otherwise all you've done is add weight to the front end of the weapon.

RIFLES: SEMI-AUTOMATIC

Moving on, let's talk about semi-automatic rifles. The "black rifle," which was a nickname coined for the M16 but has come to include virtually all M16/AR-style rifles, is an excellent weapon. Many people see it strictly as a combat weapon, although I do know some folks who think it makes a good hunting rifle. For rifles in general, the .308 caliber weapons see more use for hunting than the .223 caliber weapons. Oddly enough, and mostly I imagine due to ammo count, for combat purposes the weapons are predominantly chambered for .223. Understand up front that if this is your disaster weapon of choice any government representative you encounter is going to think you've got the rifle for violent purposes instead of hunting or strictly self-defense. Why? It is an unfortunate side effect of media impact on our perceptions. After all, when was the last time you saw a television show or movie where someone used an AR-style rifle for hunting? They're always portrayed as combat weapons.

That said, plenty of semi-automatic rifles are available that don't resemble the M16/AR-style weapons in any way beyond having a shared caliber. Such weapons are typically viewed as hunting weapons, although they can easily and efficiently serve as defense weapons as well. I still recommend choosing a weapon either in .223 or .308. Here's why... in a disaster situation, you may find yourself needing more ammo. To increase your chance of finding the ammo you need for your particular weapon, choose a common caliber. Now, I know some folks who argue the other way. Their outlook is that, in a disaster, LOTS of people are going to be looking for .308 and .223 and therefore those ammo supplies will run out fast, making it more desirable to have an uncommon caliber weapon.

Most of the folks I know who HAVE set up a "crisis kit" and have included a "black rifle" have at least five to seven magazines loaded in magazines and ready to go. That's 150 to 210 rounds of ammo. It might be a little while before they have to find more. Certainly if you see your rifle primarily as a defense weapon, you're going to want more rounds available. If you see your rifle primarily as a hunting tool, then your .30-06 bolt gun or .30-.30 lever action rifle will serve admirably well. You have to identify your greatest perceived need and equip yourself for that eventuality. Know the strengths and weaknesses of the system you choose and include them realistically in your crisis planning. (More on bolt guns further down.)

You may simply want a rifle available but don't depend on it for defensive purposes. In selecting your rifle, you should have predetermined the **primary** usage you anticipate: defense or hunting? There are some rifles made today that are ideal for hunting, especially small game, and can be used for defense, although the caliber doesn't lend itself as well as some others. The rifles I'm talking about are AR-7s: collapsible *survival* rifles in .22lr. The strengths are that they completely fold down into the stock which floats. They chamber the .22lr cartridge which is cheap and easy to buy a good stock of. The weight is low, and the collapsed package can be carried easily in a pack or strapped to a pack. They come standard with iron sights, and if you're going to add on a scope of any kind (which some folks like to do), you need to recognize that the scope will not store in the stock and you'll be stuck carrying a relatively fragile piece of equipment separately.

RIFLES: SEMI-AUTOMATIC (HANDGUN CALIBER)

What some people refer to as "carbines": there are plenty of shoulder fired weapons available today in handgun calibers: 9mm, .40S&W, .45ACP and others. In fact, I've just become aware of an AR-style rifle that is being made available in 9mm and that was designed to use Glock magazines. There are some strengths and weaknesses to such a design (handgun caliber "rifle"). The weaknesses are limited range and reduced delivered energy. In other words, when you start out with a cartridge that delivers less energy (handgun ammo instead of rifle ammo), then what you're delivering down range is obviously reduced as well. The effective range of such weapons is also significantly less than that of rifle caliber weapons. Where a skilled shooter with a .308 might be able to take down game (or other target) at 1,000 yards, with a handgun-caliber "rifle," you're only going to get 150-200 yards, and the game you take down will have to be smaller because of the reduced energy delivered on impact.

The strengths are part mental and part ammunition convenience. The mental part is this: if you have a member of your family who is not a highly skilled shooter but whom you want to have a long gun in a disaster situation (I anticipate mostly for defense), then perhaps a handgun-caliber "rifle" is the best choice. It will give them greater defensive reach but will have reduced recoil and greater accuracy than a handgun in the same caliber. The ammunition convenience is this: if that shooter's handgun and "rifle" are the same caliber *and use the same magazines,* then you've reduced the complexity of your "load out" planning. For example, my wife's primary handgun is a Glock 17 in 9mm. If I acquire an AR-style weapon in 9mm that accepts those Glock magazines, then she doesn't need to carry separate magazines for each weapon. She can simply carry an adequate supply of Glock 9mm magazines and use them in either weapon as the situation dictates. Make sense?

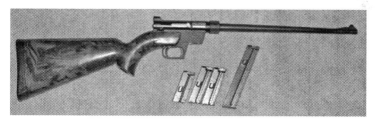

The Henry Survival AR-7 .22lr rifle. This rifle comes apart and collapses to store in the stock — which floats.

RIFLES: BOLT ACTION

When we discuss bolt action weapons, we need to recognize that some of them are excellent for hunting small game and (obviously) they do well for PROactive defense purposes. What do I mean? Well, a typical sniper rifle in .308 isn't really a defensive weapon, but snipers routinely neutralize enemy threats before the threat gets close enough to become an issue. In a crisis situation, you can't just start shooting people at a distance to keep them from becoming a threat up close. But rifles in calibers usually considered great for "plinking" (.22lr or .22Magnum) would make great food-procurement weapons while serving OKAY as defense weapons. The problem with a bolt gun as a defense weapon is two-fold: limited ammo available in the weapon and slow reload/repeat fire capability.

The example I'll use is the Marlin Model 25 in .22Magnum. Depending on what magazines you have, you either have 7 or 10 rounds in the weapon. Put on a decent scope and you've got a good rifle for hunting squirrel, rabbit, etc. The .22Mag round CAN do enough damage to be a decent defense weapon, but you've got to bolt-load every shot, and you'd better have plenty of preloaded magazines.

The other end of that spectrum is a precision built .308 bolt action weapon specifically designed for 1,000 yard+ accuracy as required for offensive military application. That bolt-action .308 is certainly a fantastic hunting tool for large game and would serve well to remove threats from a great distance. The challenge we would have in a disaster situation would be explaining to any authority after the fact how we saw someone several hundred yards a way as a threat. Keep in mind that simply because a disaster has occurred, not everyone walking around is an enemy or a threat.

RIFLES: LEVER ACTION

Another weapon that is similar in function to the bolt-action weapon and just about as ammo capacity restrictive, is the lever action rifle. Although many of us think of western movies and cowboys when we see these, the truth is that they are excellent hunting weapons, and more than one person has considered them as effective rifles for police use – even in contemporary times. You can get them chambered either for rifle calibers (.308, .30-.30, .444 Marlin and more) OR you can get them chambered for handgun calibers (.357 Magnum, .44 Magnum, etc.).

As was discussed above about handgun-caliber rifles, if you are planning your disaster weapons and want to simplify your ammunition needs, matching your rifle to your handgun can make sense. In this case, if your primary defensive sidearm (handgun) is going to be a revolver or semi-auto chambered in .357 Magnum or .44 Magnum (or other caliber available in a lever action rifle), then it makes sense to have a rifle in that caliber. The potential accuracy of a lever action rifle is excellent, and, even with the magnum handgun ammunition mentioned, you can reach out to 300 or 400 yards effectively. With rifle caliber lever actions, you're usually limited to five to seven rounds of ammo capacity in the tubular under barrel magazine, but with handgun calibers, you can sometimes get ten or more rounds in the magazine depending on the caliber and the barrel length. Additionally, in a post-disaster situation, law enforcement officers might perceive these lever-action weapons as less "aggressive" than an AR-style weapon. Don't get me wrong: guns are guns, and all will be seen as a threat, but your intended use of the weapon might not be so quickly assumed to be criminally violent.

RIFLES: BLACK POWDER

Although I can't say I'm a fan of black powder rifles (or handguns), I can easily see their applicability in a disaster situation. While certainly better suited for hunting than for defense, these weapons – in skilled hands – are capable of use as longer range defensive weapons. I know people who can shoot them pretty accurately at distances out to, and exceeding, 500 yards. They are certainly lethal at that range. Reloading is much slower than with any of the above mentioned rifles though, so that has to be a consideration. By the same token, if your definition of *disaster* is far reaching and you foresee a time when conventional ammunition is not available, then a black powder rifle might be a good idea. The necessary ingredients for loading one can be stored for fairly long periods of time, and the means of making projectiles isn't difficult. That said, the necessary ingredients to constantly load this weapon with, say, 250 rounds, takes up more space than the equivalent 250 rounds of contemporary metallic ammo. You have to take that into consideration as you plan your travel by vehicle or on foot.

RIFLES: AIR

Available in both .177 and .22 caliber, pump air rifles are an excellent long-term solution to having a projectile weapon or hunting tool in the event of a devastating long-term *disaster*. As long as you can find, make or improvise decent projectiles for it, the energy necessary to fire that projectile is developed by you pumping air into the system. The price of these weapons can be low – especially as compared to modern rifles – but remember that you get what you pay for. If you buy a $40 air rifle, the seals on the air system may easily break and not be replaceable. The velocity at which the projectile is fired is directly related to the pressure the air system will develop and hold prior to being released (when the weapon is fired). The higher that pressure (and therefore projectile velocity) is, the higher the price tag. If you plan to include an air rifle in your disaster planning kit, research and invest wisely. Several hundred projectiles (pellets) can be purchased relatively cheaply and don't take up a great amount of space. Since most of them are lead, however, they do weigh quite a bit given their size. As with any other rifle, the air rifle has to be carried either in hand, or slung unless you are traveling strictly by vehicle. Measure the value – both short and long term – and plan accordingly.

HANDGUNS: SEMI-AUTOMATIC

Across the span of the past few decades, great debate has been had about handgun calibers, stopping power, etc. Understand up front that handguns in general don't perform well as man-stopping weapons. Think about it: when you hunt a deer with a rifle, even if you score a good hit, you expect to track that deer a little while. Why? Because the deer isn't immediately killed. He has to bleed out. While he's bleeding out, he has oxygen in his brain and muscles to continue fleeing from the threat. We humans are no different. If you shoot a person with a rifle or handgun, unless you score a hit to the central nervous system, the person has enough oxygen in his muscles and brain to continue functioning for anywhere from ten seconds to a half hour or more. It depends on the wound and rate of blood loss.

What's that mean? It means that the difference between "big and slow" and "small and fast" is, to some extent, academic with today's bullet design technology *and depending on what your realistic expectations are*. A jacketed hollow point bullet will do fairly well for a defense round whether it's a .45 caliber bullet, a .40 caliber bullet, a 9mm bullet, a .357 or .38 caliber bullet, etc. The key to selecting a handgun in your disaster planning involves a couple of very subjective (personal) perceptions:

- ▲ What is the primary purpose? Hunting or defense? (or both?)
- ▲ What ammo is commonly available to you?
- ▲ What is your background/experience with handguns? (less experience means you should pick a simple gun)

I know men who are experienced with and knowledgeable about handguns and revolvers WAY beyond my own knowledge and experience. Even amongst themselves they disagree on what's "best." The .45 versus 9mm debate is over a hundred years old and won't stop anytime soon. In American law enforcement, the .40S&W is now the dominant caliber, but there are plenty of agencies carrying .45ACP, 9mm, .357Sig and others. World wide there is still a commonality in NATO of 9mm, but there's still plenty of .45ACP as well. Commercial sales of revolvers are still healthy, and ammo continues to be made for them at a respectable rate.

For defense, it helps to have a larger caliber weapon to some extent. A .22lr handgun isn't the greatest self-defense weapon, but it's better than having no gun in your hand at all. A friend of mine likes to say, *"The .25ACP in your pocket is better than the .45ACP in your glove compartment,"* and he's absolutely right. When the immediate threat presents itself, NOT having a gun at hand means you have no gun at all. What's the lesson? Don't get so hung up on having a large caliber handgun that you end up with something too heavy to carry or that you are uncomfortable shooting. Ultimately the effectiveness of any handgun (or other weapon system) boils down to **your** competence with and confidence in the "system:" that being you, the weapon and the ammo.

So, for defensive hand-gunning purposes you have two big choices and then multiple smaller ones. First, pick between a semi-automatic pistol or a revolver. While the revolver is a simpler weapon, semi-autos usually offer higher in-gun ammo capacity. Revolvers, on the other hand, usually offer greater versatility in ammo use. For instance, a revolver in .357Magnum can also fire .38 Special ammunition. That means one revolver with two ammo choices, doubling your chance of finding ammo you can use. A 9mm pistol shoots ONLY 9mm ammo. The strength of 9mm is that it's so common you can find it about anywhere.

If you're going to be using your handgun primarily for hunting, then a smaller caliber may be wise (assuming you're hunting small game and at close range). A .22lr handgun with a six-inch barrel would be fine for hunting squirrel and rabbit and would fit the bill for emergency defense remembering that the small bullets don't deliver a great deal of energy. If you're going to be using your handgun primarily for defense, then larger calibers such as 9mm or .45ACP would be better, but using bullets that big isn't usually good for hunting small game. So much energy is delivered that the game tends to get mangled beyond usefulness as a food source. If you're REALLY good and can stalk a deer that close, you probably could take it down with a 9mm or .45ACP round, but – again – you may end up tracking that blood trail a long way and the deer is suffering throughout. It's not the most humane choice of hunting tools. Also, if you're carrying a rifle or other long gun, then the handgun isn't your hunting tool anyway. It's a secondary weapon used in necessity and only when your primary weapon (the long gun) is either empty, malfunctioning or not otherwise available.

To carry that handgun for disaster purposes, make sure your holster matches your intended primary purpose. A quick-draw tactical holster is unnecessary for a hunting pistol. A flap-covered field holster is awfully slow to draw from for a self-defense pistol. Nylon, leather, and composite holsters abound for virtually every handgun manufactured today. Do your research before selecting your weapon, and then do the add-on research to identify the holster you'll need with it. Identify your perceived ammo needs and make sure you have a method for carrying the extra loaded magazines or speed-loaders (for revolvers) in whatever volume you decide is necessary. (See the notes in the **Disaster Planning 105: Belt & Pockets** section.)

HANDGUNS: REVOLVERS

The greatest strength of revolvers over semi-automatic handguns lies in the revolver's versatility of ammunition. Even if you have a revolver chambered for a single caliber (.38 Special as the example), you can get multiple different kinds of ammunition in that caliber. You could get good defensive semi-jacketed hollow point ammo; you could get ammo better suited for hiking protection such as shot shells for snakes. You can get "hot loaded" ammo, "target" ammo, jacketed or non-jacketed ammo, etc. Depending on the duration of the disaster in

question, there may come a point where you simply don't care what kind of ammo you have as long as you can load that handgun with something effective as a defensive load.

Again, when you select your handgun to be part of your gear for disaster planning, you need to identify what you perceive as your primary intended use for it: defense

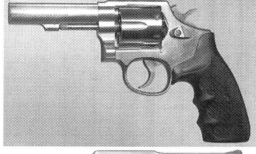

Stainless Steel .357 Magnums will fire .357 OR .38 Special ammo making them more versatile in disaster/survival situations.

or hunting? If it's defense, then make sure it's in a decent caliber for such: .38 Special would be the bottom end with .357 Magnum, .41 Magnum, .44 Special, .44 Magnum and .45 Long Colt being recommended. One of the best "disaster" revolvers available is a stainless steel (for its rugged durability) .357 Magnum either with a four- or six-inch barrel. This weapon CAN be used to hunt medium-sized game but is extremely effective as a defensive tool as well. If you can't get .357 Magnum loads for it, you can shoot .38 Special ammo out of it if need be.

If you perceive your need to be hunting focused, and recognizing the limitation to small game, revolvers in .22 Magnum with six-inch barrels work pretty well – and some come with interchangeable cylinders so that you can get a single revolver that shoots either .22lr **or** .22 Magnum. Such small caliber handguns, while well suited for small game hunting, are not ideal (or anywhere near preferred) for self-defense and should only be considered defense weapons as secondary to a good primary weapon.

HANDGUNS: BLACK POWDER

While black powder revolvers are not to be casually dismissed as defensive weapons, one has to recognize and understand the practical restrictions of their use. Where "regular" revolvers fire metallic cartridges and can be reloaded pretty quickly, the black powder revolver tends to take more time (unless you're switching out pre-loaded cylinders, and even that is time consuming). Black powder revolvers don't tend to be as accurate either. That all said, they are better than having no handgun at all. As was discussed in the black powder rifle part of this section, if you anticipate the *disaster* lasting so long that you run out of ammo for your other weapons, then having a black powder revolver or two stored away "just in case" might not be a bad idea. Of course, you also have to store the powder, caps, balls, wads, etc. While this might be viable if you are sheltering in place or traveling exclusively in your vehicle, if you're on foot and carrying all your supplies, this simply won't be practical *unless* these revolvers are your *only* choice in handgun.

BOWS, CROSSBOWS & BLOWGUNS

Far older than any firearm, the bow, crossbow and blowgun are often laughed at when people consider disaster readiness. While I appreciate how easy it is to dismiss the concept of these tools as defensive items, I would point out a few things:

1. You can hunt and/or fish with a bow.
2. A quality crossbow delivers bolts fast enough to go *through* game (deer size).
3. A blowgun, if used skillfully, can bring down small game easily.
4. As defensive tools, bows and crossbows both can reach out to 100 yards with ease.

So, taking all those things into consideration, do we still cleanly dismiss them? How about the cost of ammo and reloading? While neither a bow nor a crossbow is as compact as a rifle (although some might argue that) and the ammo isn't as easy to carry (some would argue that too), both are highly effective hunting tools. They *can* be highly effective defensive tools. As long as you have a supply of bolts/arrows, you don't need to have reloading supplies or equipment. They are a lot quieter than any firearm (unless you've suppressed the firearm sound and muzzle flash) and aren't as readily perceived as a weapon of violence by law enforcement officials. When you take all that into account, it might be wise to include one in your disaster planning. Admittedly, if you're having to travel on foot, they are cumbersome to carry. The recommendation stands to include one if you are sheltering in place or if you are traveling by vehicle; however, if no firearms are available, or if your only firearm is a handgun, then having a bow or crossbow would extend your effective hunting range quite nicely, and if you're not carrying a rifle, then carrying a bow/crossbow isn't such a burden.

Having read through the Disaster Planning Weapons section, hopefully you've done some thinking and come to some conclusions about what you want to have in your "disaster armory." The trick to immediately effective disaster planning is this: *Identify what you have on hand that you can include in your disaster kit **now**; identify what items you want to add or upgrade; budget and schedule when you will make those additions or upgrades.* This strategy doesn't apply only to weapons. It applies to tools, knives, food, ammo, shelter, etc.

DISASTER
PLANNING
107

KNIVES
& TOOLS

One of the most basic and valuable tools you can have in your possession is a knife. Recognizing that it's probably mankind's oldest tool (after the club), it's also probably mankind's most valuable tool – after the ability to build/control fire – where survival is concerned. We don't often realize it, but the number of survival-related chores we do that require cutting are numerous.

When we get into any discussion about knives for survival purposes, many people automatically think of "survival knives." Years ago when the first Rambo movie came out, the popularity of Bowie-style knives with a serrated back edge and hollow handles exploded. Mind you that was almost 30 years ago. Since then there have been some significant changes in the metals used for such knives, differences in blade shape, sheath material, etc. One question that needs to be addressed as you select your knife, or knives, to be added in your disaster "kit" is the need of size and anticipated use.

It's important to realize that no single knife is going to do every cutting chore well. Where you need a machete to clear brush, a small pocket knife will not do at all. Where you need a knife to cut your meat, a machete will not be easily used. Those are extreme examples, but you understand. As you plan and outfit your disaster kit, you'll likely need to include several knives. Of course, if you've read through the prior sections, you understand the layered approach and appreciate that you can almost have a different knife at each layer. The challenge is when you no longer have, or don't include, a vehicle in your planning. If you have to carry every cutting tool, then knife selection becomes more of a challenge and far more important to the long-term success of your survival.

For the purpose of this section, we're going to assume that you can't drive all your gear around and limit our discussion to blades at three levels:

- ▲ Chopping
- ▲ General utility
- ▲ Fine cutting

One of the easiest ways to define the purpose of the knife/ cutting tool you're looking at is to put it into one of those categories. The *Chopping* tool will have a heavier blade than handle. The balance of the tool will be well forward of your grip. The *General Utility* knife will be more balanced with a blade length relatively close to that of the grip length. The *Fine Cutting* tool will have a small blade and likely a longer handle (than the blade) with the balance at or behind the hilt.

When one thinks of a general "survival" knife, thanks to movies and television, we tend to mentally picture a knife with a seven- inch or longer blade, serrations in the spine, a hollow handle, etc. While you can certainly find all of those design features in many "survival" knives today, I can also point out a few that have a four-inch blade (or less), hollow handles, multiple carry options, a wire saw (instead of that long serrated spine), etc. The bottom line is that the perfect "survival" blade is like the best gun in a gunfight: it's the one you have in hand (or at hand) when you need it.

CHOPPING knife: such as a machete or similar. This is best kept in your vehicle or strapped to your pack.

GENERAL UTILITY knife: can be kept/carried on your pack, belt or vest. I've seen some mounted on thigh platforms in front of or behind the handgun.

FINE CUTTING knife: can be kept/carried on your pack, vest, belt, platform or even, if it folds, in a pocket or pouch.

When you look at those carry options for each one, you can see the layers. If you read back through the previous sections and remember the Disaster Planning Pyramid, you remember that each layer up (Vehicle at the bottom is the widest; You at the top are smallest) you have less room for gear. As the room for gear gets reduced, it only makes sense that the size of mandatory tools also gets reduced. In a later section, we'll discuss *all* the tools you should have in your vehicle (or your shelter), but for the purposes of this section, let's focus on what you can carry on your person. That means on or in your pack all the way down to what's smallest in your pocket(s).

A machete or other chopping size knife (usually 10″ blade or longer) can usually be attached to your pack. It might be nice to have on your belt if you can't take or lose your pack, but with everything else you probably have on your belt, do you have room for it? Actual machetes or other bush clearing tools tend to be a tad on the large side for belt carry. On the other hand, the 10" "survival" knives I've seen aren't so bad at taking up waistline real estate.

A general utility knife with a blade length between 4"-7" can be strapped to your pack, mounted on your vest, carried on your belt or mounted on the pistol platform as discussed. If you like the idea of redundancy (as I do), you can carry more than one and increase your chances of always having at least one even if you have to drop your pack or vest.

A fine cutting knife can be as small as a pocket folder provided the handle is sufficient to grasp the knife for the task at hand. On the other hand, if your *general utility* knife has just a 4" blade and you keep it clean and sharp, then it can serve as your *fine cutting* tool as well.

In your disaster planning, I recommend that you have at least one of each. If it's at all possible and you have the space/strength to carry it, I'd recommend putting a knife of some kind at each layer of the Disaster Planning Pyramid: Vehicle, Pack, Vest, Belt, You (pockets).

Knives aren't the only cutting tool you might need. Something to chop wood is good, and a hatchet or tomahawk isn't that heavy or cumbersome to carry. I especially like the *tactical tomahawks* from K5 Tactical (website URL in **Disaster Planning 110: Online Resources**) because you never have JUST a tomahawk. You have a 'hawk, hammer and pry bar OR you have a 'hawk, fighting spike and pry bar, or you have... well, you get the idea. Remember that we earlier identified: anything with more than one use; anything with increased versatility has increased value in any disaster situation.

A shovel is also invaluable. Not only do you need it for easy construction of fire pits, you also need it for burying human waste and any trash you don't want to leave behind for people to track you by. Collapsible shovels or *entrenching tools* ("e-tools") are readily available at most outdoor supply or surplus stores. They are easy to attach to a pack or belt but (unfortunately), since they're usually of all metal construction, aren't light. I still highly recommend you have one. You can save a few ounces by replacing the hard plastic carrier with a new ballistic nylon one and in the process get easier MOLLE (MOdular Lightweight Load-carrying Equipment) mounting for the carrier.

Finally, I strongly recommend you get a good multi-tool... or two... or three. One for your vehicle; one for your pack or vest; one for your belt. The value in these tools is that they have more than one tool in a single package. It may sound odd, but you just never know when you'll need a pair of pliers, needle-nose pliers, wire cutter, scissors, etc. There are a number of quality multi-tools on the market, and respected manufacturers seem to put out new models/variants every year. Many sheaths for fixed blade knives have a "utility" pouch built into the sheath face. Put your multi-tool in there and put that knife on your belt. That way, even if you have to leave your vehicle, drop your pack and lose your vest, you still have a general utility knife and your multi-tool (which would also have a fine cutting knife in it).

OTHER TOOLS IN YOUR VEHICLE

While we've discussed, above, the need for various cutting and digging capabilities that need to be addressed with tools on your person (in some way), let's talk for a minute about tools you should have as part of your vehicle load out. No matter what kind of vehicle you have, even if it's the best four-wheel drive made, there's always a chance you'll get stuck and/or that you'll find yourself stopped by a natural or man-made barrier.

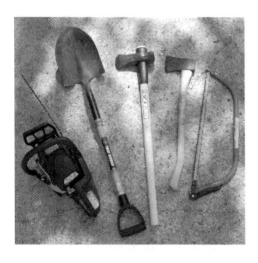

To remove such obstacles, or to help yourself get unstuck, it's recommended that you include the following in your vehicle load out:

▲ Shovel
▲ Chainsaw
▲ Rip Saw
▲ Maul
▲ Axe

A length of tow rope or tow straps is also required. Finally, if your vehicle has a place to mount it, a good winch sufficiently strong to pull your vehicle out of a ditch is an excellent idea.

DISASTER
PLANNING
108

MISCELLANEOUS

W hile the previous sections have covered the various layers of preparedness, some items haven't been discussed, the possession of which in a disaster situation may prove of value to you. Let's take a look at some of them and some things we should keep in mind when selecting any of them to include either on our person or in amongst our kit.

WATCHES

Sure, in an emergency situation where you're either constantly on the move or you're living without electricity, much of your day is planned around simple daylight. When is the sun coming up? When is it setting? Do you have lighting tools for the hours of darkness? Do you need to exercise light discipline (keep the lighting minimal) for security reasons?

If that's how you're living in an emergency or disaster situation, then watches may well be optional, however, we – as humans who have gotten used to 24 segments in a day that we call *hours* – often feel some level of stress if we just don't know what time it is. A watch is a simple solution and one that most of us wear every day anyway. But is your daily-wear watch what you need in a disaster or emergency situation? Let's think about a few things…

While I'm a big fan of the watches from MTM Special Ops, they are all electric and require an outlet to plug the recharging stand into. I regularly wear my MTM Hawk and enjoy the lighting options it includes, but if I'm living in a powerless environment, then when the batteries die the watch is useless until I can recharge it. For such situations, an auto-winder that winds itself based on movement or an electric watch that is recharged via solar energy while you wear it are better choices. Short of that, a standard digital watch with few bells and whistles is probably your best bet. Many of them run on commonly available "hearing aid" batteries. One word of caution though: if the emergency or disaster is severe enough and lasts long enough, you may not be able to find replacement batteries at your local retail outlets. Have a couple on hand and store them properly so you can change out the battery when you need to.

POCKET WEATHER TRACKERS

It is common for people to watch the news each morning and see the weather predictions (best guesses). It's also common for people to get online and look at weather websites or simply the weather widget on their main screen; however, if there's no electricity, no cable, no connectivity for your computer… how do you know what the weather's going to do?

For hundreds of years, man has predicted the weather based on whether or not the winds are moving faster (or slower), what the environmental pressure is (high or low pressure system) and the level of humidity in the air going up or down. In today's world, you can get some handy, relatively compact pocket weather "stations" that share that information (and more) with you. While I don't consider one mandatory in your preparedness kit, it's certainly convenient to have if you're educated enough to know what the various indicators mean and how to combine them to form your own weather predictions.

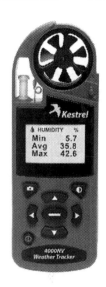

GPS

As much as I believe in redundancy, the good thing about a GPS unit is that it knows where you are and can show you where you want to go based on the information you provide. The down side is that if the batteries die you'd better have a compass and maps that you know how to use on hand.

There is an assortment of GPS units available commercially both in handheld and vehicle mounted variations. There are even wrist-worn models that are just a little bigger than your average watch. One model from Suunto will track your movements as you travel from Point A to Point B and, when you push the right buttons, feed you back your exact opposite travel so you can go from Point B back to Point A along the same route even if you don't remember it or don't recognize the landmarks.

The challenge with any GPS unit for vehicular travel is that our country's roadways are constantly evolving. If you get a GPS unit you're going to depend on for accurate travel directions, it needs to either have on-going updates as part of whatever service you pay for OR it needs to have the proper software options so you can update it via a commercial service on the Internet. The bottom line is that if the maps it uses are two or three years out of date it may be telling you to turn on roads that don't exist or taking you into places that didn't USE to be densely populated but now are. Misinformation in any emergency or disaster situation is bad.

COMPASS & MAPS

The fallback position for when your GPS dies or proves unreliable is a good compass and recent maps. The challenge many people face is that they don't know basic navigation so they can't orient the map to their position or the map to their compass or where they are to where they want to get. Whether you use GPS or not, learn the appropriate skills so you can operate without it.

As part of your travel preparedness, especially where evacuation from your residence is concerned, you should have current maps for your entire route. If you're going one state over, you need maps for your home state and the state you're going into. If you're going from New York to Colorado, you need road maps for both of those states and every one you'll drive through along the way. Additionally, if you're driving a four-wheel-drive capable vehicle and anticipate that you might have to go off-road at all (always just assume you might have to), then you'd be well advised to have topographic maps along your route as well. While road maps show you roads (hopefully with some level of accuracy), topographic maps reflect elevation, grade and (usually) are more accurate in showing bodies of water and direction of flow. They are mandatory if you're going to be traveling 4×4 style OR on foot.

MESS KITS

Across the span of the past few decades, virtually every country in the world has an army or other branch of military that has developed and/or selected a *mess kit*: that kit which provides a soldier with a pan, dish, utensils and cup. It is meant to be cooked in, eaten out of and stored away neatly and compactly after cleaning.

A decent surplus mess kit can be found at nearly every gun show and surplus store. New ones are available in a plethora of designs and features at most outdoor/camping stores and in the sporting goods section of many large retail outlets.

The surplus kit I prefer has a frying pan with a fold out handle (that

Surplus and simple: all you need in a mess kit to cook in and eat off of

locks the kit shut when folded), a two-segment "dish" (this is also the lid for the frying pan if needed), a spork (a spoon at one end, fork at the other, and knife on one side of the fork) and a collapsing cup. While not overly large, the frying pan is large enough to heat up a can of beans or soup or to fry a hamburger or slab of meat. The dish has two equally sized segments which lends itself to having a meat and vegetable or other division of foods. The ONLY challenge I see with this particular kit is that I can't hold the meat in place with the fork and use the side of the fork to cut. That said, I'm never at a shortage of knives, and I have one at each layer of preparedness that would be appropriate for cutting said meat.

HANDY DANDY

Recently I found a solar-powered recharging system that allows the users to recharge cell phones, etc., using the sun's energy. Such is potentially valuable IF you have cell service and IF you are stationary long enough to permit it to work.

During recent power outages thanks to a hurricane that passed nearby, my family found itself using the Eton solar-powered, crank-rechargeable radio quite a bit to get news and information. The solar charging panel built into the radio can also be used to recharge cell phones and the like if you're sitting still long enough. The limitation that exists is you can't listen to the radio while using the solar power system to recharge anything. The solar power system will only either run the radio OR recharge another device. Not both at the same time.

I recently saw a seat-back mounted rifle mount system that carries two long guns hanging horizontally across the back of your car or truck seats. While traveling any distance under circumstances where you want the guns reachable but not in your hands, this presents a usable option.

A company called *Spartan Tactical Concepts* makes a platform that is essentially a blank MOLLE slate. You can mount any pouches on it as you see fit. The platform itself can be hung on a seat back, carried like a backpack, or hauled off using the carry handles to hold it like luggage. The versatility offered from the three different transport options and the ability to completely customize it with pouches to suit your needs makes it of potential high value in your preparedness planning.

A roll of duct tape (sometimes called "100mph tape") can be invaluable at times, as can a bag of small zip ties. Never discount the value of a few (a dozen or so) safety pins.

DISASTER
PLANNING
109

CHECK LISTS

ncluded in this section are the published check lists from
FEMA, a published check list for camping and my own
check lists for each layer of disaster preparedness. Use them
strictly as reference material and build YOUR check list(s) to
suit your need(s).

FEMA CHECK LISTS:

FEMA suggests that you complete each list for your home,
vehicle and work. Their logic is that you never know where
you're going to be when an emergency occurs. One caveat
the author places on the "work" list: Only if you can secure it
reasonably. Spending your dollars to prepare your workmates
because they are too lazy or unmotivated to do it for themselves
is unacceptable.

FIRST AID SUPPLIES

- ☐ Adhesive bandages, various sizes
- ☐ 5" x 9" sterile dressing
- ☐ Conforming roller gauze bandage
- ☐ Triangular bandages
- ☐ 3"x3" sterile gauze pads
- ☐ 4"x4" sterile gauze pads
- ☐ Roll 3" cohesive bandage
- ☐ Germicidal hand wipes or waterless, alcohol-based hand sanitizer
- ☐ Antiseptic wipes
- ☐ Pairs large, medical grade, non-latex gloves
- ☐ Tongue depressor blades
- ☐ Adhesive tape, 2" width
- ☐ Antibacterial ointment
- ☐ Cold pack
- ☐ Scissors (small, personal)
- ☐ Tweezers
- ☐ Assorted sizes of safety pins
- ☐ Cotton balls
- ☐ Thermometer
- ☐ Tube of petroleum jelly or other lubricant
- ☐ Sunscreen
- ☐ CPR breathing barrier, such as a face shield
- ☐ First Aid Manual

NON-PRESCRIPTION & PRESCRIPTION MEDICINE KIT SUPPLIES

☐ Aspirin and non-aspirin pain reliever

☐ Anti-diarrhea medication

☐ Antacid (for stomach upset)

☐ Laxative

☐ Vitamins

☐ Prescriptions

☐ Extra eyeglasses/contact lenses

SANITATION & HYGIENE SUPPLIES

☐ Washcloth & towel

☐ Towelettes, soap, hand sanitizer

☐ Toothpaste, toothbrushes

☐ Shampoo, comb, and brush

☐ Deodorants, sunscreen

☐ Razor, shaving cream

☐ Lip balm, insect repellant

☐ Feminine supplies

☐ Mirror

☐ Contact lens solution

☐ Toilet paper

☐ Small shovel (for digging latrine)

☐ Disinfectant and household chlorine bleach

☐ Medium-sized plastic bucket with tight lid

☐ Heavy-duty plastic garbage bags & ties

EQUIPMENT & TOOLS

- ☐ Portable, battery powered/solar radio &/or television
- ☐ NOAA Weather radio
- ☐ Flashlight & extra batteries
- ☐ Signal flare
- ☐ Matches in a waterproof container
- ☐ Wrench, pliers, shovel and other tools
- ☐ Duct tape and scissors
- ☐ Plastic sheeting
- ☐ Whistle
- ☐ Small canister, ABC-type fire extinguisher
- ☐ Tube tent
- ☐ Compass
- ☐ Work gloves
- ☐ Paper, pens and pencils
- ☐ Needles and thread
- ☐ Battery-operated travel alarm clock
- ☐ Manual can opener
- ☐ Mess kits or paper cups, plates and plastic utensils
- ☐ All-purpose knife
- ☐ Household liquid bleach to treat drinking water
- ☐ Sugar, salt, pepper
- ☐ Aluminum foil and plastic wrap
- ☐ Resealable plastic bags

- ☐ Small cooking stove and a can of cooking fuel
- ☐ Games
- ☐ Cards
- ☐ Books
- ☐ Toys for kids
- ☐ Foods

FOOD & WATER

- ☐ Water
- ☐ Ready-to-eat meats, fruits & vegetables
- ☐ Canned or boxed juices, milk and soup
- ☐ High energy foods (peanut butter, jelly, granola bars, etc.)
- ☐ Vitamins
- ☐ Special foods for infants or elderly or special diets
- ☐ Cookies, hard candy
- ☐ Instant coffee
- ☐ Cereals
- ☐ Powdered milk

CLOTHES & BEDDING SUPPLIES

- ☐ Complete change of clothes
- ☐ Sturdy shoes or boots
- ☐ Rain gear
- ☐ Hat and gloves
- ☐ Extra Socks
- ☐ Extra Underwear

- ☐ Thermal Underwear
- ☐ Sunglasses
- ☐ Blankets/sleeping bags & pillows

DOCUMENTS & KEYS

- ☐ Personal Identification
- ☐ Cash and coins
- ☐ Credit cards
- ☐ Extra set house and car keys
- ☐ Copy of birth certificate
- ☐ Copy of marriage certificate
- ☐ Copy of driver's license
- ☐ Copy of Social Security Card
- ☐ Copy of Passport(s)
- ☐ Copy of will(s)
- ☐ Copy of deed(s)
- ☐ Inventory of household goods
- ☐ Insurance papers
- ☐ Immunization records
- ☐ Bank & credit card account numbers
- ☐ Stocks and bonds
- ☐ Emergency contact list & phone numbers
- ☐ Map of the area
- ☐ Phone numbers of potential places you'd go

CAMPER'S CHECK LISTS:

PERSONAL EQUIPMENT LIST

- ☐ Sleeping bag and/or blanket
- ☐ Foam pad/air mattress
- ☐ Duffle bag/foot locker
- ☐ Laundry bag
- ☐ Compass
- ☐ Canteen/water bottle
- ☐ Water purification tablets
- ☐ Mess kit
- ☐ Eating utensils
- ☐ Flashlight & extra batteries
- ☐ First Aid Kit
- ☐ Pocket Knife
- ☐ Insect repellent
- ☐ Snake bite kit
- ☐ Sunscreen
- ☐ Waterproof matches
- ☐ Emergency candles
- ☐ Soap Dish
- ☐ Toothbrush & holder
- ☐ Biodegradable soap
- ☐ Whistle
- ☐ Mirror (can be used as a signaling device)

- ☐ Rope/cord
- ☐ Sewing kit
- ☐ Tarp/ground sheet
- ☐ Playing cards
- ☐ Camera and film
- ☐ Axe
- ☐ Quarters for emergency phone calls

GROUP/FAMILY EQUIPMENT LIST

- ☐ Tent
- ☐ Extra tent pegs
- ☐ Stove
- ☐ Lantern
- ☐ Extra fuel/mantles
- ☐ Dining canopy/screen house
- ☐ Rope
- ☐ Water carrier
- ☐ Insulated cooler
- ☐ Pots and pans
- ☐ Coffee pot
- ☐ Trash bags
- ☐ Solar shower(s)
- ☐ Portable toilet
- ☐ Biodegradable toilet tissue
- ☐ Camp grill
- ☐ Air pump

☐ Folding shovel

☐ Cyalume light sticks

☐ Camp toaster

☐ Griddle

☐ Whisk broom

☐ Folding table

☐ Lantern/stove stands

☐ Salt & pepper shakers (filled)

☐ Tablecloth

☐ Fuel funnel for liquid fuel

☐ Pot holders

CLOTHING

☐ Sweat shirt(s)/pants

☐ Rain poncho

☐ Socks

☐ Hat

☐ Bandana

☐ Thermal underwear

☐ Thongs/shower sandals

AUTHOR'S LAYERED PREPAREDNESS PYRAMID CHECK LISTS:

HOME (SHELTER IN PLACE):

GENERAL:

- ☐ Water trap storage
- ☐ Water filtration system/treatment needs
- ☐ Generator
- ☐ Fuel storage for generator
- ☐ Woodstove
- ☐ Three to five cords of cut/split wood for stove
- ☐ Candles
- ☐ Strike-anywhere matches
- ☐ Prescription medications
- ☐ Spare eyeglasses for every wearer
- ☐ Books, games, cards, etc.
- ☐ Extra toilet paper
- ☐ Extra paper towels

FOOD:

- ☐ Canned vegetables, soups and broths
- ☐ Dry pasta, rice
- ☐ Canned/jarred sauces
- ☐ Assorted "camp" dehydrated food
- ☐ Assorted Heater Meals

- ☐ Vacuum-stored coffee, sugar, pepper, salt
- ☐ Vacuum-stored flour
- ☐ Vacuum-sealed jars of honey (three or more)
- ☐ Snack, Protein or Power bars
- ☐ MRE's

FIRST AID:

- ☐ Band-aids (assorted sizes)
- ☐ 2" gauze (several rolls)
- ☐ 4" gauze (several rolls)
- ☐ Triangular bandages (minimum 3)
- ☐ 2"x2" gauze pads
- ☐ 4"x4" gauze pads
- ☐ ACE bandage (minimum three)
- ☐ Sling
- ☐ Fixed or inflatable splints
- ☐ Sterile water
- ☐ Antiseptic wipes
- ☐ Krazy glue (two tubes)
- ☐ Aspirin and/or non-aspirin pain relievers
- ☐ Burn blanket
- ☐ Surgical tape, 2" width, roll
- ☐ Cotton Swabs
- ☐ Suture Kit (if properly trained)
- ☐ Blood pressure cuff (w/ extra batteries if automatic)

VEHICLE:

MANDATORY "CAMP" KIT:

- ☐ Camp Stove
- ☐ Propane tanks for stove (minimum 5)
- ☐ Propane lantern w/ stand
- ☐ Duel Fuel Coleman Lantern
- ☐ Tripod for Lantern
- ☐ Spare mantles for lanterns
- ☐ Fuel funnel
- ☐ 1-gallon can lantern fuel
- ☐ Candle lanterns (2)
- ☐ Spare Candles (minimum 6)
- ☐ Fire Starter Kit (strike anywhere matches, starter material)
- ☐ 8'x12' tarp
- ☐ Entrenching-tool (folding shovel)
- ☐ Hatchet
- ☐ "Kitchen bag" (pots, pans, plates, griddle, utensils, etc)
- ☐ 5-gallon collapsible water jugs w/ taps (6)
- ☐ 5-gallon solar showers (2)
- ☐ Small First Aid Kit (bandaids, snake bite kit)
- ☐ 12qt Tupperware container for cleaning dishes/ sink
- ☐ Aluminum stakes (16)
- ☐ Utility cord (25' minimum)

FOOD STUFFS:

☐   Heater Meals

☐   Dehydrated camp food on hand

☐   All canned/jarred goods in pantry

☐   All dry foods in pantry

☐   All snack/protein bars on hand

☐   All dry/instant oatmeal/Cream Of Wheat on hand

☐   6-person dome tent

☐   Backpack/Go Bag for each family member

☐   House first aid kit

TOOLS:

☐   Shovel

☐   Axe

☐   Chainsaw

☐   Ripsaw

☐   Maul

☐   Fuel/oil for chainsaw

HUNTING/FISHING/DEFENSE:

☐   Rod & Reel sets, tackle box (for each person if available)

☐   Extra (not family member specific) rifle(s) and ammo

☐   Extra (not family member specific) handgun(s) and ammo

☐   Pellet Rifle w/ pellet tins

BARTER MATERIALS:

- ☐ Miscellaneous ammo on hand
- ☐ Bag of knives

BACKPACK:

MOUNTED ON:

- ☐ SOG Team Leader II Knife
- ☐ RAT HEST knife
- ☐ K5 Tactical Hawk Spike (tomahawk/hatchet/pry bar)
- ☐ Snug Pak Sleeping bag
- ☐ 100oz hydration system (mounted in pack)

MAIN COMPARTMENT:

- ☐ MREs (3)
- ☐ Entrenching tool
- ☐ Boonie Cap
- ☐ Change of clothes
- ☐ Extra socks
- ☐ Extra underwear
- ☐ Gloves
- ☐ Waterproof bag (with clothing items listed in it)
- ☐ Poncho Shelter Kit
- ☐ Mess Kit
- ☐ HydroPhoton SteriPen
- ☐ Emergency Poncho (2)

- ☐ Emergency Space Blanket
- ☐ Knife sharpening Kit

SECOND COMPARTMENT:

- ☐ AMK Sportsman First Aid Kit
- ☐ SWAT-T Tourniquets (2)
- ☐ Lensatic Compass
- ☐ Micro-binoculars

THIRD COMPARTMENT:

- ☐ Fire Starter Kit (strike anywhere matches, starter material)
- ☐ Water germicidal tablets

VEST:

- ☐ Utility Pouch: emergency poncho, emergency blanket
- ☐ Extra magazines: AR-15 (3)
- ☐ Extra magazines: S-A 1911 (3)
- ☐ Extra magazines: Kahr CW4543 (2)
- ☐ Buck Hooldum Survival Knife
- ☐ Leatherman Multi-Tool
- ☐ Extreme-Beam Alpha-Tac light
- ☐ Kahr CW4543

BELT / PANTS:

- ☐ Springfield Armory 1911 .45ACP
- ☐ Spare magazine

- ☐ Cold Steel Recon Tanto knife
- ☐ PEL-6 Secutor Flashlight
- ☐ Utility pouch w/ Battle Pak First Aid kit
- ☐ Zippo Lighter
- ☐ Emerson Commander folding knife
- ☐ Wallet w/ ID, credit cards, cash
- ☐ Badge wallet / ID
- ☐ KA-BAR TDI Folding knife
- ☐ Case pocket knife
- ☐ Keys
- ☐ HawkHook Rescue Tool

WEAPONS:

- ☐ Winchester Model 94 Lever Action .30-.30 Rifle
- ☐ Springfield Armory 1911 .45ACP

FIRST AID KIT:

(house first aid kit – see previous for contents list)

ARMORER'S KIT:

- ☐ Bore snake for each weapon carried
- ☐ Pistol rod(s)
- ☐ Rifle rod(s)
- ☐ Cleaning patches (assorted sizes/calibers)
- ☐ Tor-x driver set
- ☐ Assorted sizes slotted- & Philips screwdrivers
- ☐ Replacement sights (Glock)
- ☐ Replacement firing pins (each weapon)
- ☐ Miscellaneous spare parts

ONLINE
RESOURCE
LIST

WEBSITES:

K5 Tactical	http://www.k5tactical.com
BLACKHAWK!	http://www.blackhawk.com
Survival Blog	http://www.survivalblog.com
Warrior Training Group	http://www.warriortraininggroup.com
Spartan Tactical Concepts	http://www.spartantactical.us
VooDoo Tactical	http://www.voodootactical.com
Condor Tactical	http://www.condoroutdoor.com

ARTICLES:

Blizzard Bug Out Updates	http://www.newamericantruth.com/2010/02/blizzard-bug-out-updates/
Bugout Bag Updates 2009	http://www.newamericantruth.com/2009/09/bugout-bag-updates-2009/
Go Bag 2008	http://www.newamericantruth.com/2008/05/go-bag-2008/
Backpack vs. Bugout Bag	http://www.newamericantruth.com/2007/04/back-pack-vs-bugout-bag/
Camping Under "Austere" Conditions	http://www.newamericantruth.com/2006/10/camping-under-austere-conditions/
The Bugout Bag	http://www.newamericantruth.com/2005/03/the-bugout-bag/
The Poncho Hooch	http://www.newamericantruth.com/2007/05/the-poncho-hooch/
Borelli's Rules	http://www.newamericantruth.com/2010/03/borellis-rules/
Individualized GOOD Kits	http://www.newamericantruth.com/2010/12/individualized-good-kits/
Disaster Weapons	http://www.newamericantruth.com/2007/08/disaster-weapons/
What's In Your Bag?	http://www.newamericantruth.com/2005/03/whats-in-your-bag/
"Go To Hell" Bag	http://www.newamericantruth.com/2009/07/go-to-hell-bag/
Still Serviceable Surplus Kit	http://www.newamericantruth.com/2008/10/still-serviceable-surplus-kit/
Building A Basic Survival Kit	http://www.newamericantruth.com/2008/07/building-a-basic-survival-kit/
The 9mm Option	http://www.newamericantruth.com/2010/09/the-9mm-option/
12g Specialty Munitions	http://www.newamericantruth.com/2010/08/lightfield-home-defender-specialty-munitions/

The Complete Armory	http://www.newamericantruth.com/2009/08/the-complete-armory/
Blow Out Kits	http://www.newamericantruth.com/2007/01/blow-out-kits/
The Perfect Survival Blade	http://www.newamericantruth.com/2009/07/the-perfect-survival-blade/
"Survival" Blades	http://www.newamericantruth.com/2009/02/survival-blades/
Workhorse Knives	http://www.newamericantruth.com/2007/07/workhorse-knives/
Oh Crap Gear	http://www.newamericantruth.com/2010/01/oh-crap-gear/

EQUIPMENT REVIEWS:

Extreme Beam's Alpha Tac	http://www.newamericantruth.com/2010/11/extreme-beams-alpha-tac/
Brite Strike EPLI	http://www.newamericantruth.com/2011/07/brite-strike-epl1-light-review/
AMK SOL Core Lite	http://www.newamericantruth.com/2011/05/amk-sol-core-lite/
The Buck Hoodlum	http://www.newamericantruth.com/2011/06/the-buck-hoodlum-knife-review/
Kestrel 2500 Weather Meter	http://www.newamericantruth.com/2011/05/kestrel-2500-handheld-weather-meter/
Heater Meals	http://www.newamericantruth.com/2010/12/heater-meals/
SteriPEN Water Purifier	http://www.newamericantruth.com/2008/01/steripen-handheld-water-purifier/
Henry AR-7 "Survival" Rifle	http://www.newamericantruth.com/2007/04/henry-ar-7-22lr-survival-rifle/
SnugPak Sleeping Bag	http://www.newamericantruth.com/2005/09/snugpak-sleeping-bag-32-degree/
Black Powder Weapons Today	http://www.newamericantruth.com/2007/12/black-powder-weapons-today/
BP .44 Revolver Redi-Pak	http://www.newamericantruth.com/2007/10/traditions-black-powder-44-revolver-redi-pak/
ArmaLite AR-10T	http://www.newamericantruth.com/2006/05/armalite-ar-10t-308-rifle/
Marlin Model 25 Rifle	http://www.newamericantruth.com/2006/04/marlin-model-25-rifle/
Winchester 94 .30-.30 Rifle	http://www.newamericantruth.com/2005/08/winchester-model-94-lever-action-30-30/
Remington 870 Shotgun	http://www.newamericantruth.com/2005/05/remington-870-shotgun-tried-true/
Glock 17 Gen 4	http://www.newamericantruth.com/2011/03/glock-17-gen-4/

S&W Mdl 64 Revolver	http://www.newamericantruth.com/2006/12/smith-wesson-model-64-ss-38-revolver/
Gerber Epic Field Knife	http://www.newamericantruth.com/2010/07/gerber-epic-field-knife/
RAT HEST Knife	http://www.newamericantruth.com/2009/12/rat-h-e-s-t-knife/
KA_BAR Becker Tac Tool	http://www.newamericantruth.com/2009/02/ka-bar-becker-tactool/
Razorback TROCAR	http://www.newamericantruth.com/2008/12/blackhawks-razorback-trocar/
SOG Team Leader Survivor	http://www.newamericantruth.com/2008/04/sog-knives-team-leader-knife/
K5 Tactical Tomahawks	http://www.newamericantruth.com/2008/03/tomahawks-from-k5-tactical/
Mil-Tac M3 Knife	http://www.newamericantruth.com/2008/02/new-m3-knife-from-mil-tac/
Luminox Field Test	http://www.newamericantruth.com/2011/02/luminox-field-test/
Café 2 Go	http://www.newamericantruth.com/2010/11/cafe2go/
MTM Hawk Watch	http://www.newamericantruth.com/2010/03/mtm-hawk-watch/
Delia Tactical Raptor Tool	http://www.newamericantruth.com/2009/06/delia-tactical-raptor-tool/

ABOUT THE AUTHOR:

FRANK BORELLI is a military service veteran with experience as a Military Policeman, an Infantry soldier and a Combat Engineer. In addition to his military service, he's spent all of his adult life – approximately 30 years as this text is prepared – working in law enforcement and training officers/deputies how to survive high-risk situations.

This book marks his seventh published book: five non-fiction and two fiction, in addition to two research papers that have been published.

Frank accepts emails with comments, criticisms and observations to frankborelli@officer.com.